Carol Spenser's
Style
Directions
for Women

PIATKUS

I dedicate this book to my
daughter, Hattie, who must
always remember that
a winning smile and
bubbly personality *will* go
a long way...

© 1999 by Carol Spenser

First published in 1999 by
Judy Piatkus (Publishers) Ltd.,
5 Windmill Street, London W1T 2JA

This paperback edition published in 2001

The moral right of the author has been asserted

A catalogue record for this book is available from the British Library

ISBN 0 7499 1955 8 hbk
ISBN 0 7499 2095 5 pbk

Designed by Jerry Goldie
Data capture and manipulation by
Create Publishing Services, Bath
Printed and bound in Great Britain by
Bath Press (Glasgow) PLC

Acknowledgements

My heartfelt thanks to all the following individuals and companies who have enthusiastically supplied advice, pictures, products or their talents for this book:

Piatkus Books – Judy Piatkus, Philip Cotterell, Gill Bailey and especially Rachel Winning whose frantic messages on my ansaphone I will miss terribly.

Margaret Bateman – my amazing secretary who after six years, six books and 10,000 Mail-Order-Makeovers is still going strong! (Tele: 01223 812737)

Jerry Goldie – for the fantastic design and layout of this book – and his extreme calm and patience at all times. (Tele: 020 8891 4886)

Hilary Kidd (a.k.a Willy) – for the beautiful illustrations which she somehow deciphered from my efforts.

Amway (UK) – Jean-François Heurtas, Sharon and Andy Norman, Caroline Porter and Sharon Harrison for their enthusiastic support of my Style Directions concept; for cosmetic and skincare information in Chapter 5; and for use of Artistry cosmetics and the Amway Accessories Collection in Chapter 8. (Tele: 01908 363000)

Michelle Attlesey – for all her help and expert skills with the Artistry cosmetics for Chapter 8 – great results.

Clynol – for the loan of two of their top UK hairdressers: Gary Hooker for most of the hairstyles featured in the book (Tele: 0191 217 0217); Paul Falltrick for the fantastic hair makeovers in Chapter 8. (Tele: 01708 442266)

Tony Chau – photographer extraordinaire for his talents and good humour on our photo-shoot for Chapter 8 (we especially loved his dancing!). (Tele: 020 7241 4810)

House of Fraser – for supplying the majority of the fashion photos in this book – especially Dan Harper in the press office for all his help. (Tele: 020 7963 2000)

Debenhams – for many other fashion photos in this book – especially Shirley Mitchinson, Personal Shopper at Debenhams Oxford Street London, for a fantastic supply of clothes for the makeovers in Chapter 8. (Tele: 020 7408 3827)

Bianca – especially their PR supremo, Karen Berman, for supplying some beautiful outfits for Chapter 8. (Tele: 020 8959 2374)

Freemans – mail-order fashion company for the makeover outfits on pages 17, 140 and 157. (Tele: 0800 900 200)

Alexon/ Ann Harvey/ Eastex – especially Helen Wiltshire in the press office for supplying many pictures from the above ranges. (Tele: 01582 723131)

Boots Opticians – for the wonderful array of glasses featured in Chapter 2. (Tele: 0121 236 9501)

The Body Shop – for photos and information on black and Asian colourings featured in Chapter 4. (Tele: 01903 731500)

Next – for swimsuit picture on page 50. (Tele: 08702 435435)

Bally – for supplying a fantastic range of footwear for Chapter 8. (Tele: 020 7287 2266)

Makeover Volunteers – last, but definitely not least, an extra special thank you to all the ladies who took part in our makeover days for Chapter 8 – great sports who really made my job so enjoyable.

Note – the exact merchandise/services featured in this book may not be available at the date you purchase and read the book. Please contact the above companies for details of their current ranges. All colours are subject to the limitations of the printing process.

Chapter

1

Image
Directions

One of the most enjoyable and rewarding aspects of my job as a style consultant is seeing the results of the many makeovers I perform for magazines, newspapers and television. Back in the early 1990s, when I founded my business, I decided to revolutionize the traditional format of the makeover by showing the effects it could have on the subject's family and friends and, more importantly, on the person's own confidence and self-esteem. The real reactions to a wonderful new image were never normally seen by the general public, as they occurred 'behind the scenes' after the cameras had been put away. The message I wanted to make clear, by incorporating everyone involved in the person's lifestyle, is that attention paid to your 'outer' self can pay huge dividends to your 'inner' self and future prospects. Many people's lives changed for ever.

As this message got across through my regular 'Style Counsel' makeovers, my postbag became increasingly filled with letters and photos from people of all ages, shapes and sizes, request-ing that chance to have their looks and lives revamped! Many were from women who bemoaned the lack of attention from their 'other halves'. For instance:

Above: Attention to your 'outer' self can pay huge dividends to your 'inner' self and future prospects.

> 66 *Please, please could you try and make my husband have some kind of reaction to me. I was once getting ready to go out and asked him how I looked (meaning my make-up). He said, 'Oh, all right but you need a belt on your dress' – only it wasn't a dress but a long winceyette nightie! I'd love for him to say 'You look lovely' or even a simple 'Nice' would do. We've been married nearly fourteen years and I haven't managed to get him to react. Do you think you could get him to respond to me? He does love me but has a funny way of showing it!* 99

Sandra, Nottingham

Another frequently mentioned topic was the effect of children. It appears that when some women become mothers they transfer all their time, money and attention to the new arrival – only to regret it at a later date when they see the effect it has had on their looks, confidence and self-esteem:

> 66 *Since Daisy came along all I ever wear are jeans and T-shirts. Daisy has all the best clothes! I want to know how to look good again and stop Daisy showing up my clothing. This makes me depressed but I don't know where to start.* 99

Maria, Hatfield

Stuck in a Time Warp

Young mums, however, are not the only ones with image problems! Many of the letters I receive are from older women who feel that fashion has passed them by, leaving them stuck in the style rut of a past generation – usually the period at which they felt their happiest. This is a very common problem which can leave women looking and feeling much older than they need to. Completely losing touch with fashion and make-up trends can eventually lead to a fear of making even the smallest change or trying anything new at all for fear of looking ridiculous. So a tendency to take the 'safe', familiar option develops – even with women who once keenly followed fashion:

> 66 *In my late teens and twenties I was very fashion-conscious and took a great pride in my appearance. During my thirties I began to fear being 'mutton-dressed-as-lamb' – so for the past few years I've stuck to the same clothes, make-up and hairstyle. Now I feel dowdy and frumpy while other women my age look modern and attractive. Can I regain my confidence in my fifties?* 99

Sue, Kingston, Surrey

The Power of Appearance

The common thread running through all these letters is the realization that our appearance can and does have a profound effect on our self-esteem, confidence, relationships and future prospects. Once you begin to make changes to your appearance, even small ones such as a different hairstyle, new glasses or trying a fashionable colour, you will begin to experience the effects these changes can have on other people's perception of you. This, in turn, affects your confidence and self-esteem. It can be viewed as a kind of 'circle of success', in which 'looking good' is the starting point of an on-going journey of confidence-building and self-discovery.

When you look good and know you look good, the resulting feel-good factor means that you project yourself with more confidence and authority. This conduct and behaviour will induce positive responses from those with whom you interact – family, friends, colleagues and strangers – which simply adds to your feel-good factor and starts the circle in motion once more. Positive responses also give you added confidence to make more changes to your appearance thus magnifying the circle's effects still further.

Some famous American research by Professor Mehrabian proved that appearance – that is, height, weight, colouring, clothing, hairstyle, accessories and, in the case of women, make-up and jewellery – counts for 55 per cent of someone's opinion of us. So getting all these things right counts for more than half of the total impression we make. The next 38 per cent accounts for how we present ourselves – body language, eye-contact, confidence and so on. So if you know your appearance is good, the chances are that your 38 per cent will be pretty impressive too. This leaves only 7 per cent for what you actually know or say in any given situation – frightening but true!

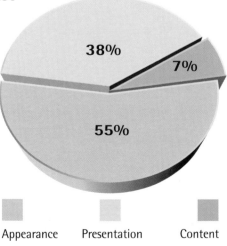

Appearance   Presentation   Content

Makeover Miracles

Changing someone's image can be a fun spot for a TV show or magazine feature and can help private individuals improve their appearance and prospects. The statistics mentioned above have, however, been responsible for some amazing transformations of public figures, which in turn have resulted in them acquiring, through a changed public response, enormous power on the world stage.

Think how Princess Diana transformed herself from a shy, blushing, teenage bride to a confident, glamorous, world ambassadress with the power to take on British royalty and win. Or of how Hillary Clinton transformed herself from a drab, bookish 'fashion-frump' to one of the most attractive, and ultimately popular, First Ladies of the USA. Or of how Margaret Thatcher transformed herself from a mumsy, housewifey minor politician to one of the most impressive,

Below: Princess Diana's amazing transformation from a shy bride (who hid behind clothes) to an uncluttered, confident world ambassadress.

intimidating world leaders of the twentieth century. None of these women could have acquired such impressive world status without changing their physical appearance along the way.

If it is true that 'You are what you wear', then by changing what you wear, as these public figures and many others have certainly proved, you can change who you are. Beginning in the eye of the perceiver, as your confidence builds it will begin to become a reality for yourself.

Silent Messages

Our appearance is therefore a means of non-verbal communication – a method of giving people infor-mation about ourselves which causes them to form opinions about us on a conscious (and sometimes subconscious) level. By changing just small aspects of our appearance – colours, accessories, make-up and so on – we can learn how to change people's reaction to us even on a day-to-day basis so that we can achieve the desired response in any situation. As an experiment, I spent half a day at a photographer's and had four different pictures of myself taken.

Groups of men and women were given one of the photos and asked to answer questions about the person, such as: How old is she? Is she married? Has she got children? What is her job? What are her hobbies? Where does she go on holiday? What are her academic qualifications? What type of house and car does she have? Opposite is a summary of some of the responses to each picture.

What is interesting about the results is that very small, subtle differences – changes in clothing, colours, styles, jewellery and make-up – together with slightly different body language and attitude, can

Picture 1
Marital status: **Married with two children (+ dogs!)**
Living location: **Gloucester/ Bath/ Cambridge**
Occupation: **Art gallery/interior designer**
House: **Restored farmhouse**
Reading: **Independent/Homes and Gardens**
Car: **Daihatsu/Discovery**

Picture 2
Marital status: **Married with one child**
Living location: **Midlands/North/ Scotland**
Occupation: **Counsellor/therapist**
House: **Victorian terrace**
Reading: **Guardian/Good Housekeeping**
Car: **Mondeo/Peugeot**

Picture 3
Marital status: **Married, no children**
Living location: **America**
Occupation: **Businesswoman/lawyer**
House: **Penthouse apartment**
Reading: **Elle/Vogue/Time Magazine**
Car: **Mercedes/BMW**

Picture 4
Marital status: **Married with two
    children (+ nanny!)**
Living location: **London/South-east
    England**
Occupation: **Advertising/PR/fashion**
House: **Mews/loft/warehouse**
Reading: **Times/Elle/Marie Claire**
Car: **Porsche/Lotus**

produce such wildly differing opinions of the same person. I could have cheated and used wigs, padding, glasses and so on to make me look completely different for each picture. What this clearly demonstrates is how an understanding of style, colour and body language can enable you to make the exact impression that you want to in any given situation, with very little effort and without a vast wardrobe. Paler colours, for example, make you more approachable than darker ones; structured clothing gives you more authority than non-structured clothing; earrings give more 'presence' than necklaces; brushed or matt jewellery gives a softer impression than shiny pieces; hands folded together are non-threatening; a hand on chin shows a listening/caring personality; hands on hips shows aggression or confidence.

So, which picture is the 'real me'? They are all me in different situations.

Picture 1 is how I look at home or on holiday.
Picture 2 is how I dress for magazine events, television etc.
Picture 3 is my image for corporate seminars or lectures.
Picture 4 is my look for dealings in the fashion world.

Once you understand your own style 'blueprint', small changes to it can make enormous differences to your image and impact.

Lifestyle Revolution

The everyday lives of men and women have changed enormously over recent years. There are now many more women in the workforce and an increasing number at extremely high levels. Men no longer feel it necessary to be the main breadwinner, and some choose to stay at home in the child-caring role. Working from home, for individuals or couples, is a rapidly increasing trend facilitated by the huge advances in communications technology. Health and fitness are becoming as important in people's lives as their job or status, and leisure/social activities are becoming more valued as lifestyles become more complicated.

In the past decades, you had one life at a time. You were a student, or a parent, or a highly paid office worker, or a lowly paid charity-worker, and you dressed according to your role in life. Today, you can be all those things at once – a parent who also works full-time in an office, studies at evening classes and does charitable work at weekends. Life is definitely more interesting and varied today, but because we all juggle so many different roles we need a wardrobe which takes us effortlessly from one situation to another. This does not mean we need a vast amount of clothes, but such a wardrobe needs knowledge and planning to provide all the essentials for an early visit to the gym; a morning working at home; an afternoon at the city office; an evening out socializing; and a weekend with the kids. Most people, particularly women, have far too many clothes and yet still encounter the 'nothing to wear' situation on an almost daily basis. The fact of the matter is that they have the wrong clothes for the type of life they now lead.

Get Sorted!

Choosing to sort out your appearance can therefore be prompted by a variety of different reasons:

- To feel happier about yourself
- To gain more confidence
- To improve relationships
- To begin a new phase of your life
- To get out of a time warp
- To change the course of your life completely
- To reflect the different roles of your lifestyle

Do you need a change of direction?

Answer the questions in the quiz below to see how much in need of change you are!

Although such quizzes can be viewed as a bit of harmless fun not to be taken too seriously, if you answer them truthfully the results can provide that much-needed 'kick in the butt' to precipitate some action.

1.	Do you regularly receive compliments?	Yes	No
2.	Do you always feel you look good?	Yes	No
3.	Do you have the right clothes for all occasions?	Yes	No
4.	Do you regularly update your hair and make-up?	Yes	No
5.	Do you keep in touch with latest fashions/trends?	Yes	No
6.	Do you ever get taken for younger than you are?	Yes	No
7.	Do you regularly try new fashion colours/styles?	Yes	No
8.	Do you treat/pamper yourself regularly?	Yes	No
9.	Do you look much different from how you did ten years ago?	Yes	No
10.	Does your appearance reflect the 'real' you?	Yes	No
11.	Do you often envy others' sense of style?	Yes	No
12.	Do you try to copy others' style without success?	Yes	No
13.	Do you make resolutions to change but never do?	Yes	No
14.	Do you use clothes/make-up to 'hide' behind?	Yes	No
15.	Do you feel guilty spending time/money on yourself?	Yes	No
16	Do you lack confidence because of your appearance?	Yes	No
17.	Do you have problems selecting items when shopping?	Yes	No
18.	Do you want to make more impact at home/work/socially?	Yes	No
19.	Do you feel you are 'beyond help'?	Yes	No
20.	Do you want to 'get sorted' but don't know where to start?	Yes	No

Your Answers to the Quiz.

If you answered mostly 'No' to questions 1 – 10 and mostly 'Yes' to questions 11 – 20,

you are in serious need of an overhaul and should start without delay. Your looks, confidence and self-esteem appear to be far lower than they should be and you should take positive steps to remedy the situation. You have nothing to lose and the only way is up!

If your answers were a mixture of 'Yes' and 'No'

at random throughout the quiz, you appear to be halfway to a successful image – some days getting it right, some days getting it wrong – but probably with no real idea why it works on some days but not on others! A clear under-standing of the secret of your best style will have you looking and feeling good 100 per cent of the time.

If you answered mostly 'Yes' to questions 1 – 10 and mostly 'No' to questions 11 – 20,

you appear to have an appearance and level of self-confidence and esteem which many would envy. As well as my regular TV and magazine makeovers, I have to date given advice to over 20,000 individuals via my mail-order makeover service (see p.158 for details) and my heart always sinks when I receive an application and photos from someone (probably like you) who already looks fantastic! I always think my advice will be rather obvious to the applicant, but I am pleasantly surprised to receive letters back thanking me for explaining why they were getting things right – for them it was an 'accident' or a natural gift rather than knowledge. Or perhaps you're a style 'guru' and this book is joining an army of other books on similar topics on your bookshelf – if so, I hope you enjoy adding to your knowledge in this ever-developing field.

The Right Direction

So whether you're in need of a complete revamp, just require a little fine-tuning in certain areas, or simply want to add more to your knowledge, this book will take you step-by-step in the right direction. By the end you will be able to:

■ Define your facelines and know how to choose glasses, hairstyles and necklines to make an impact

■ Re-evaluate your body (its good and not-so-good bits!) and select appropriate styles

■ Understand your colouring and see how different colours can project you in a different light

■ Begin to plan a wardrobe that caters for your lifestyle needs and budget

■ Follow quick and easy skincare and make-up routines to keep your face in superb condition

■ Translate the latest fashion trends into styles suitable for your age, taste and personality

Right: A change in your lifestyle – perhaps returning to work after children – is the ideal opportunity for a change of image. Sylvie Parfett wanted a more fashionable look – but not 'mutton dressed as lamb'!

Chapter

2

Face
Directions

Now that you've decided to take the plunge, reassess your looks and change your life for the better, where do you begin? You might think that your body is the biggest area of concern, but, although the body accounts for approximately seven-eighths of your total appearance, your face and everything which surrounds it make a far greater impact on your overall image – especially when you meet someone for the first time. All women are familiar with those dreaded 'bad hair' days or, even worse, a disastrous trip to the hairdresser's when a decision to try a new style can leave you in the depths of depression for several months! So, although people will take in the appearance of your figure and clothes in the first instance (interestingly, research shows that men notice your figure first, while women notice your clothes), the part of your body which receives the most scrutiny and judgement during any conversation or communication is the face. Deep down inside we know this to be true, which is why our confidence takes a knock if we feel our hair, skin, make-up, glasses and so on are not looking as good as they could be. Several women can wear the same 'little black dress' but what will make the difference between them is their choice of hairstyle, jewellery, neckline, hat or glasses which all act as a frame around the 'picture' – which is, of course, the face.

Above: Boost your confidence by knowing that your hair, skin and make-up are looking as good as possible.

To work out how to create the perfect frame around your 'picture', there are two aspects of your face which you need to understand and assess fully:

What is your face shape?

This helps you to decide on your best shapes for hairstyles and glasses.

Are your facial features soft or sharp?

This decision helps you to select your most flattering jewellery, neckline and hat shapes.

Knowing Your Face Shape

For many women, assessing their face shape seems to be far more difficult than assessing their body shape. Despite the fact that we see our naked faces several times a day in a mirror (most of us try not to see our naked bodies at all, if we can help it!) the majority of women haven't a clue whether their face is round, square or turnip-shaped! For the mail-order makeovers which my company supplies women fill in a questionnaire and send photos of their face and body shapes. Some leave the face-shape section empty; others tick several conflicting boxes; and many just write 'Help!' in the margin. I have come to the conclusion, looking at the discrepancies between the forms and the photos, that women find this task difficult for several reasons:

■ Their **hairstyle** often obscures their true face shape
■ Their **glasses** are totally wrong for their face and influence their decision
■ Their **features** may conflict with their face shape and dominate the face

First, when trying to work out the shape of your face it is very important to scrape back all your hair into a pony-tail, hairband or turban. (Men are much better at assessing their face shape, probably because their relative lack of hair makes it easier for them.) Secondly, glasses should be abandoned to enable you to make an accurate assessment. (If you are blind as a bat without them, perhaps get a loved one to make the decision for you!) Thirdly, pay no attention at all to the shape of your nose, mouth, cheeks, eyes and so on. Sometimes a woman with very soft, or even chubby, features will see her face as 'round' because of the influence of her features, even though the face shape is actually a complete square or rectangle.

With hair tied back and glasses removed, you can try to draw your face outline on a mirror if you have a steady hand. In my first book, *Style Counsel*, I recommended doing this with a lipstick or eye pencil, but after receiving many complaints about the resulting mess which needs to be cleaned off the mirror I now recommend simply dipping your finger on to wet soap! Stand as close as possible to the mirror (if not the drawn outline will be the size of a postage stamp), close one eye and trace around the entire outline of your face starting at the top. Stand back, view your handiwork and tick three boxes below:

- ❏ Does the outline curve gently all the way round?
- ❏ Or are the sides, top and jawline straighter?
- ❏ Are the length and width of your face equal?
- ❏ Or is your face longer than it is wide?
- ❏ Have you a wide forehead and a narrow chin?
- ❏ Or a narrow forehead and wider jawline?

The answers to all these questions should help you once and for all decide on your face shape and take the first step in working out your best look. Study the drawings opposite with their accompanying descriptions to see which one is closest to your face shape.

Is There a Perfect Face Shape?

It is often said that the 'oval' is the perfect face shape but, despite having one myself, I have never really liked this statement because all face shapes can look attractive and stylish if they are complemented by the right hairstyle, glasses, jewellery and so on. Yes, an oval face can look good in lots of different styles, but a square/rectangle/heart-shaped face can actually look stunning if treated positively and with confidence. Think of Jackie Onassis' square face or Liz Taylor's heart-shaped face as superb examples of self-assured personal style. Never try to copy another person's sense of style: understand and accept exactly what you are and develop your unique look on that basis.

Analyzing Your Face Shape

Curved Outlines

Oval
This face has gently curving sides and is longer than it is wide. The chin will be slightly narrower than the forehead, rather like an egg shape.

Round
This face has gently curving sides but its length and width are relatively equal, almost circular in shape.

Heart
This face has a gently curving outline but the forehead is much wider than the chin, which can appear 'pointed'.

Pear
This face has gently curving sides but the jawline is wider than the forehead, making quite an unusual face shape.

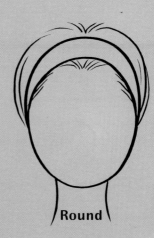

Oval

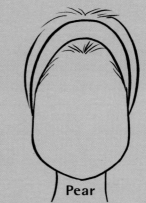

Round

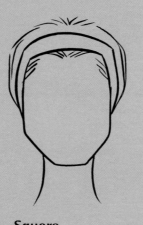

Heart

Pear

Angular Outlines

Rectangle
This face has straight sides and a square jaw and the length is longer than the width; it is often called 'oblong'.

Square
This face has straight sides and a square jaw but the length and width are relatively equal, making quite a 'short' face.

Diamond
This face has straight sides but with a narrow forehead and chin; the cheekbones are the widest point.

Choosing a Hairstyle

There are plenty of hairstyle magazines now available in the newsagents to give you a good idea of the current trends in styles, cutting and colouring techniques. Film, music and media celebrities also have a big influence on the latest fads for certain styles. Don't make the mistake, however, of cutting a picture out of a magazine and taking it to your hairdresser in the hope that

Hairstyles for Curved Outlines

Oval

I mentioned earlier that this is often regarded as the 'perfect' face shape, and it is true that an oval can take most hairstyles because it is quite a balanced face without any extreme proportions. Long or short styles look good, but sometimes long hair piled up too high on the head can cause this face shape to look a little too long unless a wispy fringe is incorporated.

Round

As this face is quite short, a heavy, straight fringe can look disastrous – a clear forehead with perhaps only a few wisps of fringe is best. A bit of height always benefits this face shape, so long hair worn up or short hair back-combed a little at the crown looks good. Alternatively, long hair which is flat on the top with an off-centre parting can give a lengthening effect at the sides of the face if the style is not too straight. Avoid hair scraped back in a severe pony-tail.

Heart

This face can easily take a volume of hair around the narrow chin area, so flicked under or flicked out bob styles are always good. Heavy, straight fringes should be avoided unless you want to emphasize the wide forehead as a point of individuality. Side fringes which break up the forehead are most flattering. Long hair looks good worn up as long as the style is not too wide, and soft tendrils dangling near the chin will balance the forehead.

Pear

As this face is the opposite of the heart shape, the opposite advice is best. A full, heavy fringe acts as a good balance to the wide jawline, and very full hair around the chin area – especially flicked out styles – should be avoided. Long hair can look good worn up, but side tendrils falling near the wide chin are not flattering. Fullness needs to be concentrated at the temples.

you can immediately acquire the latest trend or filmstar fad and automatically look fantastic. Remember that your face shape, and even the thickness and texture of your hair, play a big part in determining which styles will and will not suit you. By all means use magazines for inspiration, but bear the following guidelines in mind when snipping out pictures for your hairdresser:

Hairstyles for Angular Outlines

Square

Like the round face, this shape is very short, so a heavy fringe simply reduces the face to a very small area which can look completely swamped! A clear forehead with maybe a few wispy strands looks good, but height at the crown or long hair worn up works best. A short style, without fullness at the sides, can be very flattering if the sides are cut into choppy layers coming forward across the sides of the face.

Rectangle

For this shape, a style which gives width and fullness is good to balance the length of the face. Alternatively, if a longer, straighter style is preferred, a fringe will help reduce an over-long look. Hair worn up can be difficult as it adds to the overall length of the face, so hair taken back in a French pleat or chignon with a slight fringe is a better alternative. Above all avoid long, straight hair with a centre parting unless you wish to emphasize the rectangular look of the face.

Diamond

As this face has a narrow forehead and chin it can take fullness in either or both of these areas. A flicked out or flicked under bob style with a full fringe is therefore very flattering. Hair worn up will also widen the forehead, and tendrils look good next to the chin. A style which gives most fullness at the sides while remaining close at the forehead and cropped in at the neck can be most unflattering.

Hair Makeovers to Suit Your Face Shape

Oval
An oval face is lucky enough to suit most hairstyles.

Rectangle
A rectangular face benefits from a fringe to cut down its length.

Round
A round face always suits some height and a soft style.

Square
A square face also needs height but suits a much straighter style.

Making a Spectacle

After hairstyle, I would say that choosing glasses is the next biggest headache for women – particularly if they have to be worn all the time which makes them a very important and integral part of image and appearance. Thankfully, there has been a huge shift in attitude towards wearing glasses over the past few years, and many people now own several pairs to reflect the varying roles within their lifestyles – different styles for day, leisure and evening. Indeed, glasses have become such a fashion accessory in London that they can be bought easily and cheaply with plain glass lenses to enable those with perfect eyesight (usually the young) to blend in with their older, arty colleagues who actually need to wear them!

Glasses are therefore no longer an embarrassing sign of old age but an easy way to give yourself a stamp of individuality and style in a place where no one can fail to see it – slap, bang in the middle of your face. So if you've had the same old specs for years (yes, the big owl-like frames of the 1980s), or if you've been putting off buying a pair for fear of looking old or frumpy, get yourself down to one of the new spectacle shops without delay and have fun picking out some new, fashionable glasses. With the vast range of designer and own-label frames to choose from, you are bound to find at least a few flattering pairs which, believe it or not, can add to a stylish look rather than detract from it. Thanks to celebrities like the Spice Girls, who have made specs a fashion statement, playground taunts to children who wear glasses should become a thing of the past.

As with hairstyles, just bear your face shape in mind to find your most flatter-ing shape of frames. Even if you don't need glasses (yet!) the tips on the following pages are also useful for all women who want to find their most flattering shape for sunglasses.

Below: Glasses are no longer an embarrassing sign of old age but an easy way to give yourself a stamp of individuality.

Get Fitted

Knowing the shapes to look for is the first step in finding the perfect glasses but then ovals, squares, aviators and so on come in all different sizes and weights. Having glasses which are too big or too small for your face can destroy their desired effect, so the following tips will ensure that you are not under- or overwhelmed by your choice of specs:

Size

■ The top of the frame should not sit above your eyebrows or you will be left with a look of constant surprise! On the eyebrow is good if the frames are quite thin or do

Below: There are now glasses for all occasions – work, rest, play and evening.

not obliterate your eyebrow completely. Below the
eyebrow is best if the frames are heavy.
- The sides of the frame should not extend too far beyond
  the sides of your face or come too far in towards your
  nose. Parallel to the sides of your face is best unless you
  deliberately want to widen your face.
- The bottom of the frame should **never** sit on your cheeks
  – this is the most common problem. Not only can it
  irritate your skin but it fattens your nose and leaves your
  eye 'floating' at the top of the glasses – the 'goldfish in a
  bowl' syndrome! Ideally, your eye should be in the centre
  of the frame.

Weight

If you are petite or small-boned, lightweight plastic, delicate metals or frameless styles will look more complementary than thick, heavy varieties. Conversely, if you are large-boned, or fuller-figured, heavier styles will be more flattering; delicate, lightweight frames will conflict with your scale and make you appear bigger.

Covert or Overt?

The advice I have just given on glasses shapes assumes that

Glasses for Curved Outlines

Heart
Avoid shapes with a heavy top-frame as these will emphasize the width of the forehead. Fullness at the bottom of the glasses or low-set arms are flattering as they balance the narrow chin area. Sharp or softened rectangles look good.

Pear
A wide or heavy top to the frame is good to broaden the forehead and balance the chin. Avoid fullness at the bottom of the glasses and low-set arms which draw attention to the chin. Choose styles which are frameless at the bottom.

Oval
Most shapes of frames will suit you, so to narrow down your choice and make a definite statement use the softness or angularity of your features to help make your selection (see later in this chapter). Oval faces can often look good in frames slightly wider than the face, for instance 'cat's-eye' styles.

Round
Avoid round glasses, which will echo and emphasize your face shape. Gentle ovals or softened squares are the most flattering for you. A clear bridge will help to narrow your face, and high-set arms will add extra length.

most people want their frames to be complementary to their face. Other people – particularly creative, extrovert or showbiz personalities – will deliberately break the rules to make their glasses a dominant feature of their appearance. Putting round glasses on a round face (Lenny Henry) or square glasses on a square face (Chris Evans) often results in a comic or 'nerdy' look and therefore needs a great deal of confidence and personality to carry off! An 'overt' or 'covert' look to your glasses can also be achieved by the colour of the frames – see Chapter 4 for further details.

Glasses for Angular Outlines

Square
This face needs to be lengthened, so frames which are quite shallow, such as ovals or rectangles, work best. High-set arms will also lengthen the face, and a clear bridge will help narrow it. Coloured, patterned or contrasting vertical sides to the frames will help add to the illusion of extra length. Avoid square glasses at all costs.

Rectangle
As this face is longer than it is wide, frames which shorten or widen the face are best. Deep or square glasses work well. Low-set arms or a low bridge will also help shorten the face. If you are already shortening your face with a fringe, wide rectangles can be very flattering. If you have no fringe, however, a coloured horizontal line across the top of the glasses has a similar effect.

Diamond
Frames that will add width to the forehead and/or chin work best. If you are widening your forehead with a fringe, you may want to have glasses with fullness just at the bottom. If you are widening your chin with a bob hairstyle, frames with width at the top only may be best. If you want to widen your forehead and chin, aviator-style glasses are ideal. Avoid styles which are very wide at the cheekbones or have fancy, decorative arms, as these will further widen your face.

Defining Features

Knowing your face outline is important for achieving the right balance in the shape of your hairstyle and glasses. But for the finishing touches of jewellery, scarves, necklines, hats and so on around the face, your features now have an important part to play to complete the picture. If your features are mostly soft (Hillary Clinton) you will be most flattered by contoured shapes, patterns and fabrics around your face. If your features are mostly angular (Cherie Blair),

	Curved	Angular
Eyebrows	Curved/rounded	Straight/angular
Eyes	Full/round	Almond
Cheeks	Softer/rounded	Prominent bones
Nose	Rounded/full	Thin/straight
Lips	Rounded/full	Thin/straight
Chin	Curved/rounded	Square/pointed

First Ladies of Style (opposite):

Hillary Clinton with soft hairstyle, curved jewellery and rounded neckline (left); Cherie Blair with sharper hairstyle, angular jewellery and V-neckline (right).

- If your ticks fall mostly on the left, your features give a soft, contoured impression.
- If your ticks fall mostly on the right, your features give a sharper, straighter impression.
- If your ticks fell equally between the two, your face is a mixture and you could choose to develop either an angular or curved style around your face. To help you make this decision, use your face shape to cast the final vote:

    If it was one of the curved shapes (oval, round, heart, pear) let that be the chosen direction for your style

    If it was one of the angular shapes (rectangle, square, diamond) let that be the chosen direction for your style.

your features will be most flattered by sharper shapes, patterns and fabrics around your face. Mrs Clinton suits drapy necklines, curvy jewellery shapes, contoured hats and soft patterns on scarves. Mrs Blair, on the other hand, is more suited to sharp necklines, angular jewellery, stiffer hats and geometric patterning on scarves. Each of them would look ridiculous and uncomfortable in each other's best styles.

In the past, women with an angular face were advised to 'soften' the effect by what surrounds it. At the time of writing Camilla Parker-Bowles still does this with curly hair and frilly necklines, but the result is not flattering and she would be best to adopt a sharper, less fussy look around the face. Today it is considered more stylish and confident to 'play up' to your features than to attempt the impossible and change them – unless, of course, you resort to the plastic surgeon's knife!

Look at the descriptions on page 33 and tick the boxes which most accurately describe your features. As with defining your face shape, you may find this difficult because you are so familiar with the subject, so you may like to ask a friend or relative to help you reach your decisions.

Having a definite style around your face makes a big difference not only to how 'together' you look but from a practical point of view it makes shopping easier and wardrobe planning more flexible. For example, collars will go with other necklines; earrings will go with other necklaces; hats will complement scarves, and so on. Once you have this understanding of your features you can think back to your best shapes of hairstyles and glasses and fine-tune that selection even further by selecting the softer or more angular options for your ultimate stylish look. The chart opposite will give you some helpful tips for your future shopping decisions.

Study the photographs of the women and see how 'together' they look – although their chosen styles are completely different. This is because the lines of their face, hats and necklines are all working together to achieve a look of effortless style.

Analyze Your Features

Curved

Necklines
Rounded collars and lapels, cowl, scoop, sweetheart, shawl, pie-crust, bow, drape

Hats
Rounded crowns, soft fabrics, contoured brims, soft decorations, rounded hat pins

Jewellery
Round, oval, swirls, hoops, knots, shells, buttons, hearts, scrolls, pear-drops, tear-drops, rounded-links, round pearls, flowers

Angular

Necklines
Pointed collars and lapels, turtle, polo, V-neck, mandarin, wing-collar, square, slash, cross-over

Hats
Flat crowns, stiff fabrics, straight brims, sharp decorations, angular hat pins

Jewellery
Squares, rectangles, triangles, zig-zags, crosses, bars, trellis-work, stars, irregular pearls, cut stones, stick-drops, flat-links

Chapter 3

Figure
Directions

We're all familiar with the saying 'You can't put a square peg in a round hole', but when it comes to buying and wearing clothes many of us are guilty of trying to achieve a look which is just as impossible as forcing that square peg into the round hole. The reason is quite simple – many women don't really understand what shape they are and, more importantly, don't fully understand that certain styles of clothing are cut for particular body shapes. This was quite a surprise to me when I completed my initial style training.

The problem with understanding your true body shape arises because most women, unlike men, dwell on specific body areas (usually the problem zones!) which then cloud the total picture. For instance you may have a big bust, a prominent bottom and chubby legs and therefore think of yourself as 'curvy'. Alternatively, you may be small-busted and flat-bottomed with skinny legs and therefore think of yourself as quite 'straight'. You may focus on your big hips and thighs and define yourself as 'pear-shaped', or zoom in on a large bust and shoulders and define yourself as top-heavy. Rather than dwelling on your 'bits and pieces', you need to view your body as a whole – particularly your exterior silhouette – which from now on I will define as your Figure Direction. 'Bits and Pieces' will be dealt with later in the chapter, as they simply help to fine-tune your overall look.

Are you 'All-In-And-Out', 'Straight-Up-And-Down' or 'Somewhere-In-Between'?

Defining Your Figure Direction

In *Style Counsel* I separated women's figures into two distinctive groups: Straight and Curved. This distinction still holds true and has helped thousands of women to come to a better understanding of their most flattering styles. But since then, I have expanded my definitions to cater for those women who were perhaps slightly different types of Straight and Curved.

To analyze your own Figure Direction you need to view yourself in a full-length mirror in your underwear – high-waisted knickers are best, as they give a good impression of where your natural waistline lies. If you don't have waist-high knickers, a pair

Analyzing Your Figure Direction

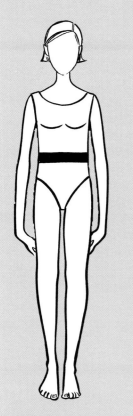

Straight
- Long, straight ribcage (can appear wide)
- Little/no waistline
- Flat hips
- Flat thighs

Tapered
- Short ribcage and/or low bust
- Visible waistline
- Rounded hips/thighs
- Hips appear high

Curved
- Long, slanted ribcage and/or high bust
- Obvious waistline
- Flared hips/thighs
- Hips appear low

Fuller
- Full bust
- Wide ribcage
- Little/no waistline
- Full hips/thighs

of tights or leggings will have the same effect. Alternatively, wear a leotard or swimsuit with a belt around your middle to define your natural waistline. Stand with your legs together and your arms a little way from your sides. Study the area from under your arms, past your bust and ribcage, over your waist and hips to the fullest part of your thighs – this is the most important part of a woman's body to understand when selecting clothing styles. Look at the four figures above to see which one is closest to your own silhouette.

Straight Figure Direction

(e.g. Princess Diana)

Your Silhouette

Although your exterior silhouette may be described as 'straight', remember that you still have a bust, waist, bottom and so on, so this figure is by no means unfeminine. In fact, many of the world's fashion models have this particular silhouette as it is one of the easiest to dress for the catwalk – fuller hips and thighs always cause fitting problems, as it is easier to take clothes in than let them out!

The main aspect of this body is that it has a straightish ribcage which appears to go immediately down into the hip bones without a big indentation at the waistline. Models with this body shape often develop an exaggerated side-to-side sway when they walk down the catwalk, which gives the illusion of curved hips when caught in photographs.

Flattering Styles

This figure is always flattered by garments with mostly straight lines and by sharply tailored, crisp fabrics and geometric patterns. If a woman with this shape is slim, she can tuck in tops and wear belts (angular buckles are best) together with pencil skirts, slim-leg trousers and short, boxy jackets. Straight dresses and coats, over-shirts and ribbed sweaters are also flattering. As the ribcage can sometimes look wide in comparison to the hips, garments with lots of waist emphasis – for instance belted jackets and skirted dresses – are best avoided as they emphasize the ribcage and draw attention away from the slim hips and thighs.

Changing Direction

If this woman puts on weight it tends to go on first around the ribcage and then the bust area, and she moves towards the Tapered Direction (see p.41). Some women with this straighter figure try to diet to achieve a 'curvy' figure with a slim waistline. If, however, you are born with a straight/wide ribcage this is virtually impossible, so a better alternative is to do exercises and work out to broaden the shoulders and develop a fuller bust. Princess Diana did this in the last years of her life and successfully achieved what appeared to be a slimmer waist when in fact she actually put on weight. You could cheat, however, and achieve the same effect with shoulder pads – much less painful! If you do build your top half, or have naturally broad shoulders, straighter styles will still look best, but you will have more ability to wear belts and 'tucked in' or slightly fitted styles.

Left: A shift dress with a short, cropped jacket is ideal for the Straight Figure Direction.

Tapered Figure Direction

(e.g. Hillary Clinton)

Your Silhouette

This silhouette definitely has a curvy outline where you can see an indented waistline and rounded hips and thighs. However, the length of the ribcage and the resulting position of the bust have an enormous impact on how much curve this figure can take in its style of clothing. Just because you have a curvy silhouette with a visible waist does not mean that you can necessarily tuck in tops tightly, wear big belts or be flattered by very fitted coats or dresses. In other words, this figure is somewhere in between Straight and Curved, and needs a style of dress with gradual waist emphasis which I now call Tapered. I have found this particular Figure Direction common amongst petite women (5ft4ins/163cm and under), myself included, who are often short in the body – especially in the depth of the ribcage.

Flattering Styles

The most flattering styles for the Tapered Figure Direction are garments such as fit'n'flare dresses, princess-line coats and semi-fitted jackets. Because of the small distance between the bust and the high hipline, wide belts should be avoided, but slim or low-slung belts can look good. Thin waistbands on skirts and trousers work well but lower-body garments with no waistband at all, which sit slightly lower on the hips, are definitely the most flattering. Tops and shirts can be tucked in, but always blouse out a little of the fabric over the lower garment to elongate the midriff.

Changing Direction

If the Tapered Figure puts on weight it usually goes on to the hips and stomach first, causing them to become even closer to the bustline. It is important to invest in good, supportive bras if you have this figure – the bustline needs to be kept as high as possible to maintain a flattering look. If a lot of weight accumulates, the Tapered Figure will move towards the Fuller Figure Direction (see p.43).

Above: A semi-fitted suit with gradual waist emphasis is ideal for the Tapered Figure Direction.

Curved Figure Direction

(e.g. Madonna)

Your Silhouette

This silhouette also has a curvy outline, but the big difference between this and the Tapered Figure is that the Curved Figure has a much longer, usually slanted ribcage which leads to a very obvious waistline and the appearance of a high bustline and lower hipline. Like the Straight Figure, this is a shape which is common amongst models and usually, because of the length of the ribcage, the owners of such Curved Figures are average height to tall – anything from 5ft4ins/163cm to over 6ft/189cm.

Flattering Styles

Because there appears to be so much space around the narrow waistline and long ribcage, the Curved Figure can take lots of waist emphasis – wide belts, peplums, full skirts and so on – without looking 'bundled up' in the middle. Straight, crisp, tailored styles are not very flattering to this figure, as they do not sit comfortably around the curves. Softer, drapy fabrics and contoured patterns work best. Because the waistline and midriff are the greatest asset of this figure, they are always best accentuated. Straighter styles which bypass the waist, particularly if they end around the hips/thighs, can make this body look fatter than it needs to.

Changing Direction

If the Curved Figure puts on weight it tends to go on evenly all over, and the measurements of the bust, waist and hips may increase considerably. However, because of the long ribcage and lower hip bones the body has the space to take the extra weight and still remain curved. Some supermodels can put on a stone or two and not look much different! If weight is accumulated over the years the Curved Figure may become Tapered (see page 41) as the bust and hips become closer, but will hardly ever become Fuller unless the weight gain is extreme.

Above: A belted safari suit in soft linen gives great waist emphasis to the Curved Figure Direction.

Fuller Figure Direction

(e.g. Sophie Dahl)

Your Silhouette

Like the Straight Figure, this silhouette has quite a rectangular shape with little waist definition. The big difference between them, however, is that the Fuller Figure is larger in all areas, either because of weight gain or simply because its owner was born with a large frame or is what women often refer to as 'big-boned'. I made a decision to include this shape as a Figure Direction in its own right (rather than as a 'proportional' issue, as is usually the case) because 47 per cent of women in the UK are now size 16 or over.

The female population is definitely becoming larger and, as long as Fuller-Figured women remain fit and their size poses no risk to their health, they should be able, by understanding their Figure Direction, to learn how to look and feel attractive and confident. Most high street and mail-order retailers have woken up to the fact that the Fuller-Figured woman accounts for nearly half of their women's wear sales, and are now producing fashionable ranges to cater for larger sizes.

Flattering Styles

Buying larger sizes, however, does not guarantee a flattering look for the Fuller Figure if the chosen styles are completely wrong. Wide, full skirts, tightly tucked-in tops and belts are best avoided altogether. It is more flattering to opt for long, straight jackets/sweaters/over-blouses/tunics over extremely straight skirts, trousers or dresses for an attractive, streamlined look.

Changing Direction

If you are in the Fuller Figure Direction at present because you are overweight, but you intend to lose weight by diet and exercise, your resulting silhouette on achieving your target is most likely to be either Straight or Tapered. Remember that the bone structure of your ribcage – its width and length – plays a big role in determining the ultimate figure you can attain. Don't however, put off making the most of yourself until you are 'slim'. Dress in the most

Above: A loose, knitted tunic-top with matching straight skirt is ideal for the Fuller Figure Direction.

flattering way for who you are now. Putting life 'on hold' for some magical day in the future often results in feelings of depression and lack of confidence causing that magical day never to arrive.

Pain-free Shopping

Now that you fully understand your Figure Direction, putting your new knowledge to use will make fashion shopping much easier. In the past you may have taken a complete hotchpotch of styles to the changing room to try on – fitted jackets, straight jackets, wide trousers, tapered trousers, pencil skirts, pleated skirts – and left the result to trial and error. You are probably familiar, also, with the frustrating situation of a size 12 fitting you for one outfit but even a size 14 not fastening properly on another! This depressing scenario results not from the fact that you've suddenly put on weight in the last ten minutes, but because the two outfits are probably cut for completely different silhouettes.

Left: Shopping becomes so much easier and quicker when you know your Figure Direction.

Garments to Suit Your Figure Direction

	1. Straight	2. Tapered	3. Curved	4. Fuller
Coats & Jackets	Chanel-style Jacket Crombie Coat Double-breasted Blazer	Zip-front Jacket Princess-style Coat Semi-fitted Jacket	Drawstring Jacket Bathrobe-style Coat Belted Jacket	Swing Raincoat Edge-to-Edge Coat Straight Jacket
Tops	Ribbed Sweater Straight Shirt Short Cardigan	Twin Set Fitted Shirt Waistcoat	Waist-welt Sweater Tie-front Shirt Belted Cardigan	Knit Tunic Over Blouse Long Gilet
Bottoms	Pencil Skirt Narrow Trousers Straight Jeans	Tapered Skirt Tapered Trousers Chinos	Gored/Flared Skirt Gathered Waist Pants Pedal Pushers	Straight Skirt Flat-front Trousers Palazzo Pants
Dresses	Shift Dress Shirtwaister Dress Evening Slip Dress	Fit'n'Flare Dress Wrap-over Dress Dipped-waist Evening Dress	Belted Dress Two-piece Dress (tucked in) Skirted Evening Dress	Column Dress Straight Pinafore Dress Evening Separates

Just as there is no point in taking a magazine picture of a celebrity to your hairdresser to achieve that same hairstyle if your face and features won't suit it, there is no point in trying to copy someone else's personal fashion style if their Figure Direction is completely different from yours. Yes, you can appreciate that your friend looks great in belted jeans with a shirt knotted at the waist, but don't try to copy it if you have little or no waistline. For a similar look, your best personal style may be a semi-fitted casual shirt over tapered chinos. Keep the blueprint of your best look in your mind whenever you go shopping; very soon, choosing garments off the rails will become as easy as pie. Furthermore, all the styles you take to the changing room should fit and suit you well, bringing your choice down to much easier decisions such as cost and colour. In fact, if you discover a garment which is perfect for you in every way, buy it in a number of colours – you won't regret it!

For a quick and easy guide to your most flattering styles, study the chart on the previous page. Some of the garments will go in and out of fashion at intervals, but the descriptions will help imprint your best kind of silhouette on your mind.

To keep up to date with the best fashions for your silhouette each season, subscribe to the bi-annual publication *'Fashion Directions'* (see page 160 for details)

Right: Keep up to date with the best garments for your Figure Direction for a fashionable as well as flattering look.

Your Bits and Pieces: Illusions with Line, Fabric, Colour and Scale

At last we come to the parts you love to dwell on! Bear in mind, however, that you've worked out the most important aspect of your body – your Figure Direction – so now all you need to know are the little tricks of the trade to draw the eye away from your not-so-good points. Let's not stop at that, though, because the following tips will also help you to draw attention to your best bits too. Don't only dwell on the negatives, but think how you can use this advice to make the most of your figure's assets.

To understand how to manipulate the viewer's idea of your shape or create illusions about certain areas of your body, you first need to have a basic understanding of how line, fabric, colour and scale can affect our perception of objects – including bodies. The most important of these four topics is line – horizontals, verticals and diagonals play a big part in our appearance.

Line

Horizontal lines

Research has shown that the eye travels down an object from top to bottom. If there are no horizontal lines across the object it normally travels quite quickly down the object and then up to the top again. However, whenever the eye comes to a horizontal line it is arrested at that point, scans across the line and then continues on its journey. Although you are not aware of it, this is what happens when you look at someone else and what happens when that person looks at you. Consequently, you never want to put a horizontal line across a part of your body that you do not like or that you do not want to draw attention to.

Most people know that horizontal stripes on a T-shirt are widening – great for the small-busted but disastrous for larger ones! It is not just stripes, however, which we need to consider when thinking about horizontal lines. Pockets have strong

Left: Any horizontal features, such as the stripes on this sweater, are extremely widening – you need a slim figure for this to be a flattering look.

Right: Any vertical features such as the ribbon-trimming on this outfit, are lengthening and slimming.

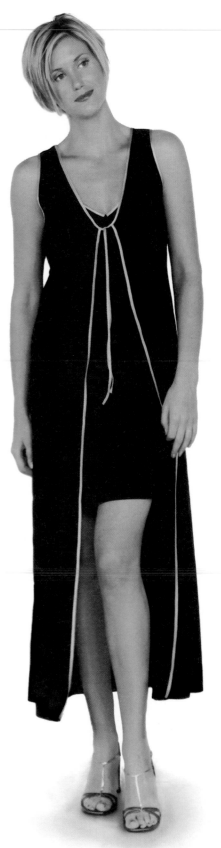

horizontal lines (avoid them on big bottoms, hips and busts) and a skirt hemline is a very strong horizontal line (always make sure your hemline crosses a slim part of your legs). The bottoms of jackets, sweaters, T-shirts and so on will all draw attention to that part of your body just like a band going round a barrel. Some necklines also have a great 'horizontal hold' on the eye, so remember that those too will spotlight and broaden your neck. Knowing where and where not to put your horizontals is vital!

Vertical lines

On the other hand, vertical lines are much more body-friendly. They accelerate the eye on its journey up and down the body almost like giving it railway tracks to

Right: The diagonal lines on this dress are semi-slimming as they fall half-way between vertical and horizontal lines.

travel on. The result is that plenty of vertical lines in an outfit will make the wearer appear taller and slimmer and, if no horizontals are present in the wrong places, most figure problems will be by-passed quite easily. If you are short and/or over-weight, stressing vertical lines in your outfit (while eliminating as many horizontals as possible) is very important. Only the very tall and/or very underweight will want to avoid too many verticals and stress the horizontal instead.

Again, do not think of verticals as just stripes on a fabric. Strong vertical lines can be created by seams, a long scarf or a strong row of buttons down the front of a garment. Some skirts, trousers and jackets have vertical pockets set into side seams which can be much more flattering than horizontal or 'patch' pockets. An outfit with an abundance of vertical lines, such as a pinstripe trouser suit (with a single-breasted jacket and no turn-ups on the trousers) worn with a long straight scarf, is one of the most slimming and lengthening looks that can be achieved.

Diagonal lines

If horizontals arrest the eye and are widening; and verticals speed up the eye and are lengthening; diagonals come somewhere in between in their ability to have these effects on your body. Basically, the closer a diagonal line comes to a vertical, the more lengthening and slimming it is; the closer it comes to a horizontal, the more arresting and widening it is. You may think that diagonals do not occur very often in clothing, but again, if you think beyond the notion of a stripe in the fabric, diagonals are quite common.

A V-neck is made up of diagonals, and therefore the deeper it is the more slimming it becomes to a thick neck. Halter-necks put diagonal lines across the shoulders and are therefore good at diminishing too broad shoulders but disastrous for narrow or sloping ones. Wrap-over-style swimsuits take the eye across and away from a large bust; asymmetric hemlines can elongate short legs; and a dipped yoke or pockets set at an angle on the back of jeans can help reduce a large bottom.

Sometimes an array of diagonal lines can be used together in a pattern to trick the eye into perceiving one part of the body as being a lot smaller than another. A swimsuit or leotard which has diagonal lines converging into a point on the waistline will make the waist look smaller than it really is – in fact, this style can create the illusion of a waistline where none exists and is very flattering for the Straight or Fuller Figure. Occasionally, diagonal lines can occur by accident with undesired results. A pleated skirt, for example, whose pleats do not hang straight down in vertical lines but fan out over large hips produces diverging diagonal lines which are extremely widening and fattening, so beware!

Above: The closer a diagonal line comes to a vertical line, the more slimming it is; converging diagonal lines are most slimming of all.

Fabric

Choice of fabric also affects focal points on the body and apparent size of various parts. As with horizontal lines, the eye is arrested by and zooms in on the bright aspects of an outfit. Because shiny fabrics reflect light and appear 'bright', they draw attention to themselves. The reflection of the light also makes the part of the body they cover appear larger. A white, silky blouse will therefore draw attention to the bust area and make it appear larger; satin trousers will enlarge the bottoms they encase; a totally shiny dress or suit will add inches to the entire body; and glossy tights/stockings can turn ample calves into two plump pork sausages! This is vital information for women who are planning a wedding, as shiny fabrics are often used in profusion. Make sure that the bride and bridesmaids aren't blown up out of all proportion by yards of shiny fabric which can look even worse in flash photography.

By now you've probably worked out that matt fabrics have the opposite effect – they don't draw the eye and can reduce the perceived size of the parts they cover. Matt fabrics absorb the light and are therefore more body-friendly for those who want to look a little slimmer. Returning to our examples above, a cotton blouse, gabardine trousers, jersey dress and matt tights/ stockings are better options if your figure is less than perfect in any of those areas.

Above: Deep colours, matt fabrics and vertical lines are all slimming or lengthening.

Right: Light colours, shiny fabrics and horizontal lines are all fattening or shortening.

Finally, on the topic of the eye being drawn to 'sheen and shine', jewellery can also be used to draw attention to or from particular areas. A brooch placed high on the shoulder draws attention away from a too large bust; a necklace hanging over a beautiful bustline draws attention to it. Bangles draw attention to elegant wrists and dangly earrings can highlight a long, slim neck. Remember that belt buckles too can be shiny objects – if you don't want too much attention focused on your waistline, fabric-covered buckles can be more flattering.

Colour

Certain colours work best next to your face according to your individual colouring and you can find these in Chapter 4, but it is also useful to know that dark colours (black, navy, brown, burgundy, pine green and so on) act rather like matt fabrics in that they absorb the light and make areas clothed in them appear smaller. Yes, that is why black is nearly always slimming – it is not a myth! If, however, the black garment is made up from a shiny fabric such as black satin it will no longer be slimming because the power of the 'shine' over-rides the power of the colour. So if you want to reduce certain areas of your body, deep-coloured matt fabrics will always be best. Everyone can wear dark skirts, trousers, jackets and coats if they are teamed with a 'personal' colour near the face.

Lighter colours (cream, beige, pink, lemon, baby blue, dove grey and so on) have more reflective qualities and therefore make areas appear larger. If you have to choose between the same dress in lemon or navy and are nervously wondering 'Will my bum look big in this?', opt for the navy one every time! If the colour is too deep next to your face simply add a lighter scarf, jacket or jewellery for a flattering effect.

Buying what is right for your body is far more important than sticking to a particular swatch of colours.

Below: A straight outfit in a deep colour
and matt fabric is ideal for the Fuller
Figure Direction.

Scale

The final bit of trickery that our eyes can play on our brain is in connection with differing sizes and scales of objects. What we have to understand is that nothing is viewed in isolation but always in relation to what is surrounding it. Look at the diagram opposite and assess which central blob is the bigger – the one on the top or at the bottom.

In fact both are the same size. The one at the top appears larger because it is surrounded by small objects; the one below appears smaller because it is surrounded by large objects.

So, how does this affect a woman's appearance? Quite simply, if you are a Fuller-Figured woman (overweight or large-boned), very small details such as patterns, jewellery, bags or hats will actually make you look larger. A petite or small-boned woman who opts for very large accessories and patterns can easily be swamped and overpowered and ultimately look smaller than she really is.

However, I have found that many larger women choose to surround themselves with small things. They do so for two reasons: not to draw attention to themselves, and in an attempt to look smaller. What they achieve is the exact opposite. A large woman needs larger-scale accessories and patterns, firstly for them to be flattering to her size and secondly to project an aura of confidence about who and what she is. Similarly a petite businesswoman will often try to make herself look bigger with a large briefcase or brooch, but small to average-size pieces are in fact needed to increase her degree of professionalism..

Above: Which central blob is the biggest?

Your best scale

- Fuller-Figured/big-boned = medium- to large-scale
- Petite/small-boned = medium- to small-scale
- Petite and Fuller-Figured = medium-scale

Figure Proportions

Armed with your knowledge of line, fabric, colour and scale, you may be able to begin working out how to highlight or diminish your good and not-so-good bits and pieces. But first study the list below and tick the boxes of the particular proportions which apply to your figure. You don't need to put a tick against all of the body areas listed. For example, if your neck is neither long nor short, or if your bust is neither small nor very large, just ignore these boxes and concentrate on the areas which you want to accentuate or disguise.

The proportions listed in the left column are generally considered desirable by most women in the Western world; the majority of Western fashion models have all these attributes, so most women like to accentuate those points. The proportions listed in the right column are generally considered more of a problem by Western women, who feel they need to disguise or diminish those areas. In other cultures, however, features such as big hips, stomach and bottom are regarded as attractive – you can therefore decide for yourself which proportions you want to highlight or reduce, depending on how you feel about your body within your own culture.

Note:

On the following pages the advice given for one proportional problem may conflict with that given for another. Follow the advice for the particular proportion that causes you most problems.

Your Figure Proportions

Tick the boxes for the particular proportions which apply to your figure.

Neck	Long	Short
Shoulders	Broad	Narrow/sloping
Bust	Small	Large
Midriff	Long	Short
Stomach	Flat	Prominent
Hips/thighs	Small	Large
Bottom	Flat	Prominent
Calves/ankles	Slender	Thick
Height	Tall	Petite
	(over 5ft7ins/170cm)	(under 5ft4ins/163cm)

Dealing with Your Proportions

Neck

Will shorten or widen:
Scarves tied highly at neckline
Necklines with bows/ties
Upturned collars
Choker-style necklaces
Polo and turtle necks
Mandarin and Nehru collars

Will lengthen or slim:
Very low necklines
Open shirts and blouses
Scarves tied at a low point
Very long necklaces
Collarless jackets without a
   garment beneath
Cowl necklines

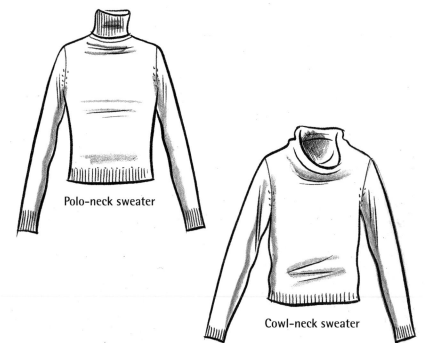

Polo-neck sweater

Cowl-neck sweater

Shoulders

Will reduce or slim:
Small or no shoulder pads
Halter necks on swimsuits and dresses
Raglan sleeves – the seam lessens the
   shoulders
Deep necklines
Thin straps on swimsuits and dresses
Set-in sleeves
Brooches worn on the lapel or near the bust

**Will broaden or balance with
   hips:**
Large epaulettes – make shoulders more
   noticeable
Details at shoulder, e.g. gathers, pleats,
   stripes, yokes
Wide-apart straps on swimsuits, dresses
   and nighties
Brooches pinned wide on the shoulder
Shoulder pads – soft are best
Cap sleeves, which flare out from shoulder
Boat or slash necklines
Off-shoulder evening dresses or
   wraps/stoles

Halter neck

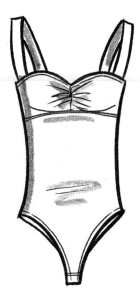

Wide-set straps

Bust

Will enlarge or draw attention to:

Bulky textures on top half to add substance

Horizontal lines/seams at bustline to increase width

Layering, e.g. cropped waistcoats over big shirt

Breast pockets add detail at bustline

Uplift or padded bra

Very low necklines

Very tight top, e.g. Lycra

High-waisted swimsuits

Checked patterns on top half

Brooches and necklaces at bust level

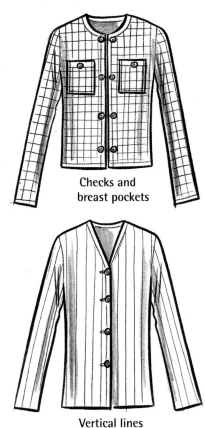

Checks and breast pockets

Vertical lines

Will reduce or slim:

Plain, matt fabrics on top half

Medium-length necklaces

Brooches on shoulder

Dolman sleeves (body and sleeve cut in one piece, very loose fitting)

Loose-fitting garments on top half

Vertical or diagonal details on top-half garments

Small or no waistband on lower garments

Minimizer bra

Higher necklines

Wrap-over swimsuits

Midriff

Will shorten or draw attention to:

Wide belts and cummerbunds

High-waisted styles on skirts and trousers

Belts in the same colour as the bottom garment

Contrasting belts or sashes

Tight tops

Top garments tucked in tightly

Blouses knotted at waistline

Knotted blouse

Blouse to be worn outside

Will lengthen or slim:

Yokes on skirts

Dropped waist styles

Garments without waistbands

Very thin belts

Hipster styles

Belts in the same colour as top-half garment

Uplift bra

Blouses worn outside or 'bloused out' over bottom garment

Stomach

Will enlarge or
draw attention to:

Shiny fabrics on stomach
Tucked in tops
Gathered or drawstring
  waists
Front-fastening trousers
  and skirts
Tops ending across
  stomach
Non-supportive
  underwear and
  swimsuits
Dropped waists or yokes
Tight skirts/trousers
Unstitched pleats/darts

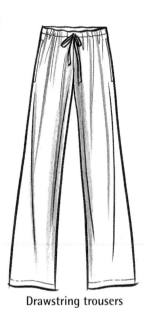

Drawstring trousers

Will reduce or slim:

Deep, matt fabrics
Bloused out tops
Flat-fronted trousers and
  skirts
Small or no waistband
Loose skirts and trousers
Side- or back-fastening
  trousers and skirts
Tops ending below
  stomach
Control panel underwear
  and swimsuits
Stitched-down
  pleats/darts

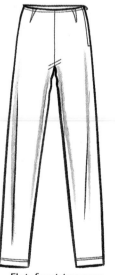

Flat-front trousers

Hips and thighs

Will enlarge or draw attention to:

Horizontal details across area
Pockets on jackets, skirts and trousers
Full skirts
Gathered or drawstring waistbands
Gathered ankles on trousers
Long shoulder bags
Shiny fabrics and light
  colours on bottom half
Short skirts and shorts
Unstitched pleats
Dropped waists and
  yokes
Short tops and jackets
Tight, short skirts,
  shorts and
  trousers
Prints or patterned
  skirts, trousers
  and leggings

Patterned, gathered skirt

Will reduce or slim:

Vertical lines on bottom half
Stitched-down pleats
Loose clothing on lower half
Shoulder pads, epaulettes, etc.
Centre pleats on skirts
Dark, matt colours on bottom
Short-strap shoulder bags
Pinstripe skirts and trousers
Lighter/brighter jewellery or
  colours on top half
Control briefs and tights
Knuckle-length tops and
  jackets
Sewn-down side pockets
Knee-length skirts and shorts

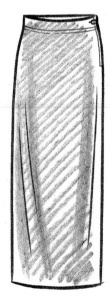

Plain, straight skirt

Bottom

Will enlarge or draw attention to:

Shiny fabrics
Light colours
Square back pockets
Straight yoke on jeans
Tops and jackets ending around
   bottom
Tightly tucked in tops
Short skirts and shorts

Will reduce or slim:

Matt fabrics
Dark colours
No back pockets
Dipped yoke on jeans
Vertical stripes
Bloused out tops
Knee-length shorts and skirts

Jeans-style shorts

Knee-length shorts

Calves and ankles

Will enlarge or draw attention to:

Light-coloured hosiery
Shiny hosiery
Delicate shoes and sandals
Ankle straps and T-bar shoes
Cropped trousers, pedal pushers,
   Capri pants
Above-knee or calf-length skirts
Calf-length or ankle boots
Ankle socks

Will reduce and slim:

Substantial shoes
Matt hosiery
Thick heels
Knee-length boots
Dark-coloured shoes
Toning tights and shoes
Broadly strapped sandals
Below-knee or ankle-length
   skirts

Delicate shoes

Substantial shoes

Height

To look shorter:

Horizontal details and stripes
Layers of garments
Different bands of colour
Contrasting belts
Dropped yoke on skirts
Border designs at hemlines
Layered necklaces, wide earrings
Medium to low heels
Wide trousers and skirts
Contrasting tights and shoes
Turn-ups on trousers
Flat shoes

Look shorter   Look taller

To look taller:

Vertical lines – stripes, seams,
   cables, etc.
Dressing in one colour
Matching tights, shoes and
   hemline
Very slim trousers
High heels
Long, narrow skirts and dresses
Long scarves and necklaces
Shorter skirts
Narrow silhouette
Shorter hairstyle
Small- to medium-scale patterns
   and accessories

4 Chapter

Colour
Directions

Readers who have come across any of my previous books will know that I have strong views on colour, and colour analysis in particular. As I mentioned in Chapter 3, I believe that style – finding the right shape for your figure and the right adaptations for your proportions – is far more important than wearing your so-called 'right' colours. During the 1970s and 1980s colour analysis was all the rage and many women became virtual slaves to swatch wallets containing small fabric samples of their 'best' colours to help them know what to choose when they went shopping. In the 1990s this practice gradually died away, and my research has found that women now want a far more flexible and individualistic approach to the subject of colour.

Above: You do not have to stay as nature intended – by colouring your hair or wearing coloured contact lenses you can dramatically alter your image.

You may have experienced a colour analysis session yourself and have perhaps been diagnosed as a 'season' – spring, summer, autumn, winter – or even a combination of seasons which 'flow' into each other. If this system works for you – if it has improved your appearance and helped you to plan your wardrobe, and you actually like the colours and can find them easily in the shops – then by all means stick with it and perhaps just read this chapter to enlarge your knowledge of colour and colourings. However, every week I receive many letters from women who have been diagnosed as different seasons by different consultants or who have grown tired of their wallet of colours or cannot find them easily in the shops.

The majority of women say that they would like some advice on selecting colours for clothes and make-up, but the system they would prefer would allow them also to wear the colours they like (including black) or those in fashion at the moment. There is nothing worse than being told you should only wear bright clothes when the current fashionable look is for muted shades or you happen not to like bright colours. Looking good and projecting confidence is much easier if you feel up-to-date and comfortable rather than old-fashioned or out of character in your colours.

Understanding Colour in General

The system which I use to determine colours for individuals, called Colour Directions, is extremely flexible as it can be applied to the new colours each season. It can also help you to wear the colours you like or to project a different look for different occasions because it explains the effect that different colours can have when teamed with your own colouring – for example, you don't always have to look 'harmonious' if you don't want to! Finally, it can help you 'change direction' if you are bored with your look – you can change your hair colour (and eye colour with contact lenses) to alter your Colour Direction if you don't want to remain as nature intended.

Before you discover your Colour Direction (or the Colour Direction you want to be), it is useful to understand a little about colour itself so that you can see how the system has been developed and how its origins are based in fact rather than fantasy.

Characteristics of Colour

Every colour has three main characteristics: depth, clarity and undertone. Once you understand the meaning of these terms and how they apply to your own colouring, finding your most harmonious (or contrasting) colours each season becomes easy – no swatch wallet is needed!

Depth

This is how deep or light a colour is. For example, charcoal grey is deep and dove grey is light. They are simply different intensities of the same colour (with many other depths of grey in between). It is important to remember that 'deep' does not mean 'dark'; 'deep' means 'strong' and 'intense'. Fuchsia pink is a deep colour (but it is definitely not dark), while baby pink is a light intensity of the same colour. In

Deep In-Between Light

fact, light colours are simply a diluted version of deeper colours – a small drop of fuchsia pink paint stirred into a glass of water would result in the baby pink shade.

Clarity

This is how bright or muted a colour is. For example, lime green is bright and sage green is muted. A bright colour is clear and vivid and reaches the eye very quickly because of its sharpness. A muted colour is soft and subtle and reaches the eye quite slowly because of its greyish, cloudy composition. Returning to our paint analogy, to turn a bright paint into a muted paint, you would add quantities of grey to lessen the clear, sharp, vivid qualities.

Bright   In-Between   Muted

Undertone

This is how cool or warm a colour is. For example, blood red is a cool red and tomato red is a warm red. What makes a colour warm or cool is varying amounts of yellow or blue within its composition. All colours contain both yellow and blue, but in differing degrees which are not always visible to the human eye. Colours with a lot of yellow, such as orange, tan and peach, are warm colours; colours with a lot of blue, such as black, fuchsia and purple, are cool colours. To make a colour warmer you would add yellow; to make it cooler you would add blue.

Warm   In-Between   Cool

If you cannot tell whether a colour is warm or cool it probably has equal (or nearly equal) amounts of yellow and blue in its composition. These are the in-between shades which are often called 'true' colours – true red, true green, etc.

Working with Colour for Yourself

Personal Characteristics

Having some understanding of colour enables you to apply those characteristics and basic terminology to yourself, because your skin, hair and eyes are all made up of pigments and colours. Melanin is a brown pigment found in skin, hair and eyes. Carotene is a yellowy-orange pigment also found in skin, hair and eyes. Haemoglobin is a bluey-red pigment in blood and is sometimes visible through the skin.

Incidentally, I always analyze a woman's colouring using the appearance she has at present rather than as nature intended, because I believe that how she has chosen to look is very much an expression of her personality. If you have decided to be a blonde or a redhead with green contact lenses, you should be allowed to be so; you should therefore receive the advice for how you have chosen to look at present. In the future you may want to change again or even revert to your natural self, but that's completely up to you. Also, the Colour Direction that you are now is not necessarily how you will stay forever. As we get older our skin, hair and eyes all fade as pigment is lost, so our colouring can change naturally from one Colour Direction to another.

Try working out your Colour Direction on this chart.

Finding Your Direction

Look at yourself in the mirror and tick three boxes: one for Depth; one for Clarity; one for Undertone.

The DEPTH of my colouring is best described as:

- [ ] Deep, strong, intense
- [ ] Light, fair, soft
- [ ] Don't know or somewhere in between

The CLARITY of my colouring is best described as:

- [ ] Bright, vivid, contrasting
- [ ] Muted, subtle, non-contrasting
- [ ] Don't know or somewhere in between

The UNDERTONE of my colouring is best described as:

- [ ] Warm, golden, burnished
- [ ] Cool, silvery, ashy
- [ ] Don't know or somewhere in between

What you have probably found is that one category was much easier to do than the other two. For example, a fair-skinned woman with blonde hair and blue eyes will tick box 2 without hesitation but may think long and hard about the other alternatives. A dark-skinned woman with black hair and brown eyes will tick box 1 easily but may ponder some other choices. A freckly-skinned redhead with green eyes will tick box 6 without qualms but perhaps query her selections in the earlier choices. This is quite normal, because it tells you something very important

Do-It-Yourself Colour Analysis – Have a Go!

DEPTH

1.DEEP (Strong/Intense)				2. LIGHT (Fair, Soft)
				X
Very	Slightly	Don't know/In-between	Slightly	Very

CLARITY

3. BRIGHT (Vivid, Contrasting)				4. MUTED (Subtle, Non-Contrasting)
			X	
Very	Slightly	Don't know/In-between	Slightly	Very

UNDERTONE

5. COOL (Cool, Ashy)				6. WARM (Golden, Burnished)
		X		
Very	Slightly	Don't know/In-between	Slightly	Very

The crosses shown on the chart are my own answers to the questions. With blonde hair (from a bottle!), blue eyes and a fair complexion, box 2 is my easiest to tick so Light is therefore my Primary Colour Direction. My colouring is subtle, with very little contrast, so box 4 is the next easiest to tick, making Muted my Secondary Colour Direction. I do not feel particularly Warm or Cool as I have golden blonde hair (warm), blue eyes (cool), and skin which is rosy in winter (cool) and freckly in summer (warm). Undertone is therefore not important to me – I can wear both warm and cool colours. What is most important is that my most harmonious colours are Light and my second best are Muted.

about your colouring – whatever box was easiest to tick is probably your Primary Colour Direction. If you found two boxes easy to tick, you've probably discovered your Secondary Colour Direction too – all you need is to put them in order.

To put your Colour Directions in order of importance draw up a chart like the one opposite, putting crosses where you feel your answers to the questions fall. Use pencil at first as you may change your mind after some thought.

Can't decide?

If you could not decide between your Primary and Secondary Colour Directions or if (yes, it does happen occasionally) you answered 'don't know' in all the categories, look at the pictures and descriptions on the following pages to find the colouring which most closely resembles your own. You will then be able to discover your most harmonious clothing colours for wearing next to your face, harmonious make-up shades and even colours for spectacle frames and jewellery to complete the picture.

I have stressed that colours only need to be harmonious next to the face – on your body, style, shape and fit of clothing are more important. Any woman can wear a black suit, but a Light woman might want to team it with an ivory blouse, for instance; a Deep woman a red blouse; and a Warm woman a peach blouse.

You can, if you choose, wear your harmonious colours from head to toe and the look will be great if the style is also right for you. Remember, however, that where colour is concerned you have the freedom to follow your own tastes or fashion trends on the major part of your body, if you so wish.

Deep Direction

Typical examples are Cher, Paloma Picasso and Oprah Winfrey. This colour pattern is the most common throughout the world, particularly in hot climates, and is often described as strong, powerful or intense. Most dark-skinned women will have Deep as their Primary Colour Direction unless they have coloured their hair blonde or red, wear coloured contact lenses (bright green or blue) or have hair which has gone grey.

Typical Colourings

Hair: black, dark to mid-brown, chestnut brown (not red)

Eyes: dark brown, deep hazel, olive green, dark blue

Skin tone: medium to dark (often tans easily).

Harmonious Colours

For near face: rich purple, forest green, burgundy, royal blue etc.

Neutrals: black, charcoal grey, dark brown, deep navy (good colours for leather accessories)

Best 'white' near face: pure white

Fashion colours each season: any deep, strong, intense colours will suit you well

Glasses Frames: deep brown, grey, black, tortoiseshell, dark metals

Jewellery: dark wooden beads, deep enamels, black pearls, shiny metals, deep stones.

Harmonious Cosmetics

Eye shadows: icy beige highlight, grey, navy, aubergine, moss green

Eyeliner/mascara: black, charcoal, navy, teal

Blusher: deep berry, burgundy, browny red

Lips: red, deep pinks, terracotta, rust.

Secondary Colour Directions

- If you are Deep but have lots of contrast between your dark hair/eye colour and a lighter skin tone, your Secondary Colour Direction is Bright (see p.72)
- If you are Deep and have mid-brown hair, medium skin tone and medium depth eyes, your Secondary Colour Direction is Muted (see p.74)
- If you are Deep but have evidence of blue/ashy tones your Secondary Colour Direction is Cool (see p.78)
- If you are Deep but have evidence of golden tones, your Secondary Colour Direction is Warm (see p.77).

Colouring Your Hair

- If you go more than 50 per cent grey you will be heading in the Cool Direction
- If you go more than 50 per cent red you will be heading in the Warm Direction
- If you go more than 50 per cent blonde you will be heading in the Muted Direction.

Opposite Colour Direction

Light (see p.71) is your opposite Colour Direction. Pale pastel shades, such as powder pink, baby blue, beige, cream and lemon are the most difficult colours for you to wear, especially near the face or as cosmetics or glasses frames. If you do wear Light shades, be aware that they will give you a non-harmonious, contrasting look. If you are quite extrovert, or like a 'high-fashion' look, they can be eye-catching and extreme – but they need a lot of style or confidence to carry off well.

Light Direction

Typical examples are Kylie Minogue, Goldie Hawn and Princess Diana. This colour pattern is very common in Western countries, particularly England and Scandinavia, and is often described as fair, delicate or soft. It is quite a natural colour pattern amongst children, but the majority of adult women who are ash or golden blonde have usually resorted to hair colourants as their hair will by then have darkened.

Typical Colourings

Hair: golden blonde, ash blonde, very light brown/mousey, yellow-grey

Eye colour: blue, green, grey, blue-grey, green-blue

Skin tone: medium to light, often does not tan easily.

Harmonious Colours

For near face: pale pink, denim blue, mint green, lavender

Neutrals: dove grey, light brown, taupe, beige, light navy (good colours for leather accessories)

Best 'white' (near face): ivory (pure white will only look good if you are tanned)

Fashion colours each season: any light, delicate, soft colours will suit you well

Glasses frames: light-framed – cream, taupe, pale grey, light metals

Jewellery: light woods, light enamels, creamy pearls, brushed metals, light stones.

Harmonious Cosmetics

Eye shadows: pink, peach highlight, taupe, grey, sage green, lilac

Eyeliner/mascara: brown, brown-black, soft navy

Blusher: soft pinks, coral, peach

Lips: pinks, coral, peach, raspberry red.

Secondary Colour Directions

- If you are Light but have bright eyes and/or extremely blonde hair, your Secondary Colour Direction is Bright (see p.77)
- If you are Light but have cloudy/pale eyes and subtle blonde hair, your Secondary Colour Direction is Muted (see p.74)
- If you are Light but have evidence of bluey/ashy tones, your Secondary Colour Direction is Cool (see p.78)
- If you are Light but have much evidence of golden/yellowy tones, your Secondary Colour Direction is Warm (see p.77).

Colouring Your Hair

- If you go more than 50 per cent steely grey you will be heading in the Cool Direction
- If you go more than 50 per cent darker you will be heading in the Bright Direction
- If you go more than 50 per cent red/copper you will be heading in the Warm Direction.

Opposite Colour Direction

Deep (see p.68) is your opposite Colour Direction. Strong, intense colours such as burgundy, dark red, black, bottle green and deep purple are the most difficult ones for you to wear, especially near the face or as cosmetics or glasses frames. If you do wear Deep shades, be aware that they will give you a non-harmonious, contrasting look. If you are quite extrovert, or like a 'high-fashion' look they can be eye-catching and extreme – but they need a lot of style or confidence to carry off well.

Bright Direction

Typical examples are Liz Hurley, Joan Collins and Princess Caroline of Monaco. This colour pattern is characterized by a contrast between hair, skin and eyes – usually dark hair with light or bright eyes. It is often also described as sharp, vivid or clear. As a natural colour pattern it is most commonly found in Celtic countries, particularly Ireland whose inhabitants are famous for their 'twinkling eyes' which stand out from their brown hair and pale skin.

Typical Colourings

Hair: black, medium to dark brown, chestnut (can be grey or blonde only if brows are dark)

Eyes: bright blue, green, turquoise, bright hazel, violet (jewel-like)

Skin tone: light to medium, may tan or burn.

Harmonious Colours

For near face: bright pink, emerald green, poppy red, peacock blue

Neutrals: black, navy, charcoal grey, nut-brown (good colours for leather accessories)

Best 'white' near face: with a tan, pure white; if pale-skinned, off white/ivory

Fashion colours each season: any bright, clear, vivid, sharp colours will suit you well

Glasses frames: deep or bright frames, shiny metals

Jewellery: polished woods, shiny enamels, white pearls, shiny metals, bright stones.

Harmonious Cosmetics

Eye shadows: icy beige highlight, navy, charcoal, turquoise, purple

Eyeliner/mascara: black, charcoal, purple, teal

Blusher: clear pink, coral

Lips: red, bright coral, fuchsia.

Secondary Colour Direction

- If you are Bright and have dark brown hair and brows, your Secondary Colour Direction is Deep (see p.68)
- If you are Bright and have mid-brown hair and brows, your Secondary Colour Direction is Light (see p.71)
- If you are Bright and have evidence of bluey/ashy tones, your Secondary Colour Direction is Cool (see p.78)
- If are Bright and have evidence of golden/yellowy tones, your Secondary Colour Direction is Warm (see p.77).

Colouring Your Hair

- If you go more than 50 per cent steely grey you will be heading in the Cool Direction
- If you go more than 50 per cent blonde you will be heading in the Light Direction
- If you go more than 50 per cent red/copper you will be heading in the Warm Direction.

Opposite Colour Direction

Muted, dusky shades such as beige, sage green, dusky rose, mustard and khaki are the most difficult for you to wear, especially near the face or as cosmetics or glasses frames. If you do wear muted shades, be aware that they will detract from your sharp, bright look. If you do not like bright colours or they are not in fashion, dressing with contrast (i.e. light and dark together) looks good.

Muted Direction

Typical examples are Cindy Crawford, Julia Carling and Jemima Khan. This colour pattern is quite unusual in adults and does not occur very frequently in natural colour patterns. Women with blonde hair and darker eyes have usually lightened their hair with a colourant. The effect is often described as soft, rich and subtle. Blonde hair with such a rich eye colour does not provide a contrast (as with dark hair and light/bright eyes), but gives a more mellow, blended look.

Typical Colourings

Hair: blonde, light brown/mousey, yellow-grey

Eyes: brown, hazel, olive green, greeny/grey

Skin tone: medium to deep, may tan or burn.

Harmonious Colours

For near face: dusty rose, sage green, air force blue, aubergine

Neutrals: soft grey, greyed navy, taupe, camel (good colours for leather accessories)

Best 'white' near face: oyster white

Fashion colours each season: any muted, soft, rich, blended colours will suit you well

Glasses frames: beige, brown, soft grey, dusky pastels, brushed metals

Jewellery: mixed woods, muted enamels, creamy pearls, brushed metals, muted stones.

Harmonious Cosmetics

Eye shadows: beige or peach highlight, mink, grey, sage, plum

Eyeliner/mascara: brown, grey, soft navy

Blusher: peach, salmon, browny pink

Lips: toffee, beige, dusky pink, soft red.

Secondary Colour Directions

■ If you are Muted and have light brown hair and eyes, your Secondary Colour Direction is Deep (see p.68)

■ If you are Muted and have light hair and light hazel eyes, your Secondary Colour Direction is Light (see p.71)

■ If you are Muted and have evidence of bluey/ashy tones, your Secondary Colour Direction is Cool (see p.78)

■ If you are Muted and have evidence of golden/yellowy tones, your Secondary Colour Direction is Warm (see p.77).

Colouring Your Hair

■ If you go more than 50 per cent dark you will be heading in the Deep Direction

■ If you go more than 50 per cent steely grey you will be heading in the Cool Direction

■ If you go more than 50 per cent red/copper you will be heading in the Warm Direction.

Opposite Colour Directions

Bright, sharp, clear colours such as fuchsia pink, royal blue, emerald green and scarlet are the most difficult for you to wear, especially near the face or as cosmetics or glasses frames. If you do wear bright shades, be aware that they can be overpowering to your subtle look. If you are quite extrovert, or like a 'high-fashion' look, they can be eye-catching and extreme – but they need a lot of style or confidence to carry off well.

Warm Direction

Typical examples are the Duchess of York (Fergie), Rula Lenska and Nicole Kidman. This golden, burnished, fiery colour pattern is often associated in its natural state with northern countries, particularly Scotland, and is characterized by an abundance of the pigment carotene in the hair and eyes and often on the skin as freckles. You may, however, have dyed your hair to a shade of red (auburn, copper, ginger and so on) which, if it is a dominant aspect of your appearance, will make Warm your Primary Colour Direction.

Typical Colourings

Hair: red, auburn, copper, ginger, sandy/strawberry

Eyes: brown, hazel, bright blue/turquoise, green

Skin tone: golden or very pale, often burns easily and may have freckles.

Harmonious Colours

For near face: tomato red, turquoise, apple green, peach, coral

Neutrals: brown, camel, tan, marine navy, rust, terracotta (good colours for leather accessories)

Best 'white' near face: creamy white

Fashion colours each season: any warm, golden, fiery or burnished colours will suit you well

Glasses frames: brown, tortoiseshell, beige, golden metals

Jewellery: all wooden pieces, warm enamels, creamy pearls, silver with warm stones.

Harmonious Cosmetics

Eye shadow: beige or peach highlight, brown, teal, copper, green, turquoise

Eyeliner/mascara: brown, brown-black, teal

Blusher: apricot, peach, nutmeg

Lips: terracotta, salmon, coral, orange, warm red.

Secondary Colour Directions

■ If you are Warm and have dark red hair and dark eyes, your Secondary Colour Direction is Deep (see p.68)

■ If you are Warm and have light red hair and light eyes, your Secondary Colour Direction is Light (see p.71)

■ If you are Warm and have bright red or ginger hair or bright blue or green eyes, your Secondary Colour Direction is Bright (see p.72)

■ If you are Warm and have light red hair with darker eyes, your Secondary Colour Direction is Muted (see p.74).

Colouring Your Hair

■ If you go more than 50 per cent dark and have brown or hazel eyes you will be heading in the Deep Direction

■ If you go more than 50 per cent dark and have blue, turquoise or green eyes you will be heading in the Bright Direction

■ If you go more than 50 per cent blonde and have brown or hazel eyes you will be heading in the Muted Direction

■ If you go more than 50 per cent blonde and have blue, turquoise or green eyes you will be heading in the Light Direction.

Opposite Colour Direction

Cool, icy or bluey colours such as white, baby-blue, pale pink, fuchsia and lilac are the most difficult ones for you to wear, especially near the face or as cosmetics or glasses frames. If you do wear cool shades, be aware that they will give you a non-harmonious, contrasting look. If you are quite extrovert, or like a 'high-fashion' look, they can be eye-catching and extreme – but they need a lot of style or confidence to carry off well.

Cool Direction

Typical examples are Queen Elizabeth II, Germaine Greer and Barbara Bush. This silvery, icy, ashy colour pattern is often associated with older women whose hair has gone grey or white – not yellow-grey. Some women, however, can go grey at quite a young age or choose to go grey with hair colourants. Some hair colours, such as ash brown or brown hair going grey, have so little warmth that they too can also fall within the Cool Direction. Our research has shown that this Colour Direction comprises only a small percentage of the female population, as most women who go grey colour their hair and therefore change their Colour Direction.

Typical Colourings

Hair: white, steely grey, ash/greyish brown

Eyes: blue, blue-grey, greyish brown

Skin tone: pale, rosy or ashy, with very few freckles; can be deeper if brown-eyed.

Harmonious Colours

For near face: royal blue, cerise, bluey greens, icy lilac, blood red

Neutrals: any grey, any navy, rose brown, mink, black

Best 'white' near face: pure white (if deep complexion) or soft white/ivory

Fashion colours each season: any cool, icy or bluey colours will suit you

Glasses frames: pink, blue, silver grey, gunmetal

Jewellery: wood mixed with silver, black and white pearls, silver, platinum, cool stones.

Harmonious Cosmetics

Eye shadows: icy beige, pink highlight, navy, grey, lilac, plum

Eyeliner/mascara: black, navy, plum

Blusher: rose pink, berry

Lips: raspberry, rose, bluey red, wine.

Secondary Colour Direction

- If you are Cool and have darker hair and eyes, your Secondary Colour Direction is Deep (see p.68)
- If you are Cool and have light hair and eyes, your Secondary Colour Direction is Light (see p.71)
- If you are Cool and have lots of contrast in your colouring, e.g. bright eyes and dark brows, your Secondary Colour Direction is Bright (see p.72)
- If you are Cool and have light hair with darker eyes, your Secondary Colour Direction is Muted (see p.74).

Colouring Your Hair

- If you go more than 50 per cent dark and have brown eyes you will be heading in the Deep Direction
- If you go more than 50 per cent dark and have light eyes you will be heading in the Bright Direction
- If you go more than 50 per cent blonde and have dark eyes you will be heading in the Muted Direction
- If you go more than 50 per cent blonde and have light eyes you will be heading in the Light Direction.

Opposite Colour Direction

Very yellowy colours such as orange, lime green, egg yellow and tan are the most difficult for you to wear, especially near the face or as cosmetics or glasses frames. If you do wear warm shades, be aware that they will give you a non-harmonious, contrasting look. Subtle warm shades such as beige, lemon, sage, khaki etc. can look good (see above) especially with a coral pink lipstick.

Black and Asian Colour Directions

Women of African, Afro-Caribbean or Asian background will nearly always have Deep as their Primary Colour Direction because of their dark hair and eyes and, often, darker skin tone. Deep, strong intense colours for make-up and clothing near the face will always be more flattering (very pale, or pastel shades will create a contrasting, arresting or 'high-fashion' look). Knowing your Secondary Colour Direction is, however, extremely important if you are a Black or Asian woman, so that you can fine-tune and personalize your look in an individual way. Study the pictures and descriptions below to find your Secondary Colour Direction from the four listed:

Deep and Bright

This colouring is characterized by a lot of contrast between dark hair and eyes and a paler skin tone – which can range from the ivory/porcelain skin tone of Oriental women to the light brown/beige of darker skins. The Deep colours outlined on page 68 will suit you well but look also at the bright shades on page 72 to expand your options. Combining Deep and Bright colours together will always look good. If you do not like bright colours, contrast in your clothing (e.g. black and white) and clarity in your make-up (e.g. sheer lipstick) will always look good.

Deep and Muted

This colouring is characterized by a lack of contrast between the skin, hair and eyes giving a soft, mellow, blended look. The hair is usually not very dark, the eyes can be hazel or mid-brown and the skin is usually medium in depth. The deep colours outlined on page 68 will suit you well but look also at the muted shades on page 74 to expand your options. Combining Deep and Muted shades together will always look good. Aim to blend your clothing colours together and select matt rather than shiny shades of cosmetics and jewellery.

Deep and Warm

This colouring is characterized by an overall 'golden glow' which emanates from the hair colour, eye shade and skin tone. The hair can be a rich golden brown or subtle red highlights can be visible in darker hair. If the hair colour is natural, the eyes will usually be a hazel or golden brown colour and the skin may sometimes have freckles – especially in summer. The Deep colours outlined on page 68 will suit you well but look also at the warmer shades on page 77 to expand your options. Combining Deep and Warm colours together will always look good, together with gold or wooden jewellery and warm-toned cosmetics.

Deep and Cool

This colouring is characterized by an overall 'bluey or ashy' look which emanates from the hair colour, eye shade and skin tone. The hair can be an ash-black, blue-black or even be beginning to go grey. The skin can also have an ashy or bluey look or even a 'rosy' tone to the brown. The eyes can be very dark – almost black – or may have a greyish tinge to the brown shade. Usually, there is very little evidence of warm or golden tones. The Deep colours on page 68 will suit you well but look also at the cool shades on page 78 to expand your options. Combining Deep and Cool colours together will look good, together with silver jewellery and cool-toned cosmetics.

Chapter 5

Beauty Directions

Beauty today is not about having a classically beautiful face – it is about feeling good as well as looking good. Making the most of yourself and projecting a healthy and confident glow is now considered more important than being just a 'pretty face'. Looking after yourself, however, needn't break the bank or necessarily mean several hours a day spent in the bathroom! If you understand which products and techniques are best for you as an individual looking good should develop into quick and easy routines. Don't, however, get stuck in a rut. Just as your body shape and colouring can change over the years, your beauty routines may need to adapt to the changes in your skin, features – and eyesight!

Skin

Believe it or not the skin is the largest organ in the body, measuring almost 20 square ft/1.9 square metres in total! The skin on your face and neck is some of the most delicate on the whole body and, since it is a living thing, it must be fed and nourished in the same way as any living organ if it is to remain healthy. Looking after your skin is not just 'pampering' or 'spoiling' yourself – it is as important as looking after your heart or lungs.

Above: Making the most of yourself and having healthy glowing skin and hair is now considered more important than being just a 'pretty face'.

Stucture

It helps to know about the structure of the skin. Firstly, it consists of three layers: the sub-dermis, dermis and epidermis. The total depth of all three measuring about one-twentieth of an inch (just over one millimetre). Each layer plays an important role in keeping your skin healthy

■ The **sub-dermis** is the layer of fatty tissue that cushions the skin above it.

■ The **dermis** is the middle layer of skin which contains collagen (a super-protein that gives skin its bounce) and elastin (the substance that gives skin its flexibility and durability). The dermis also contain blood capillaries, nerves, hair follicles, sweat and sebaceous (oil) glands.

- The **epidermis** is the top layer of skin. Although incredibly thin it performs the most critical of all functions, cell renewal, which slows down considerably as we get older.

The Enemies of Skin

Babies and children have wonderful skin and need do very little to it except cleanse it properly and protect it from the elements. As we get older, however, natural changes occur in the body's chemistry which affect the function and appearance of the skin. For women, the three most important times are:

- **Adolescence:** shifting hormonal levels and increases in oil gland production make the skin especially susceptible to blemishes, spots and blackheads. Specialist skincare products are needed to cleanse and reduce the oiliness of the skin.
- **Adulthood:** the oil glands become less active, so the skin becomes drier and less susceptible to blemishes (hooray!). However, it loses elasticity, resulting in the beginning of fine lines and wrinkles. At this stage it becomes essential to start using moisturizing creams to rehydrate the skin and make lines less noticeable.
- **Post-menopause:** shifts in hormonal levels combined with less efficient renewal of skin cells and reduced production of collagen can cause the skin to become very dry and fragile, with an even greater likelihood to sag and wrinkle. Rich night creams and products containing collagen are invaluable during this period.

Our skin is also at the mercy of environmental factors which we must try to avoid or control as much as possible

Sun Possibly the most damaging of environmental factors is the sun. Its rays stimulate the skin's production of vitamin D, providing a feeling of warmth and well-being and often a deceptively healthy-looking tan. However, over the years continued exposure to the sun's ultra-violet rays will dry out, damage and wrinkle the skin considerably. The incidence of skin cancer is now also one of the fastest-growing types of cancer in the world.

Humidity Low humidity, often caused by central heating, robs the skin of essential moisture. High humidity, on the other hand, can cause the sweat glands to work overtime, making the skin feel oily. Even though skin may feel oilier in hot and humid weather, it still needs moisturizing to guard against the drying effects of the sun.

Temperature Cold temperatures, combined with low humidity, increase moisture loss from the skin, leaving it tight and dry. But hot temperatures with low humidity also remove moisture from the surface, literally 'baking' the skin. Extreme heat and cold can, therefore, both damage the skin.

Wind Strong wind, especially combined with extreme temperatures and low humidity, can cause dry and flaky skin. Also, wind-borne dust and dirt can strike the skin and stick to the surface, clogging the pores and choking the skin.

Pollution Smog and other pollutants can stick to the skin, clogging-up the pores.

Controlling sun, wind, humidity, temperature and pollution may seem beyond our personal control, so all we can do is use the best products available to combat those elements. Some factors affecting our skin are, however, totally within our control and can make a huge difference to our skin's health and appearance.

Sleep This is the simplest and most basic remedy for the skin. As we sleep, our skin renews itself by building new cells,

Above: Although the sun can produce a feeling of warmth and well-being and a 'healthy-looking' tan, continued exposure to its harmful rays without effective SPF products will damage the skin irrevocably.

so getting the proper amount of sleep each night is essential. Seven to eight hours a night is recommended for healthy-looking skin – why else is it often called 'beauty sleep'?

Water We need fluids to enable the body to flush all the impurities from its system. Drinking six to eight glasses of water (approx. 1.5–2 litres) every day can help to improve the circulation and speed cell growth. Drinking plenty of water also, surprising though it may seem, helps prevent water retention and bloating and can help with weight loss.

Nutrition Food provides all the vitamins and minerals the body needs to function properly. There is definitely a direct correlation between healthy skin and good nutrition, so it is extremely important to eat a balanced, healthy diet. An unbalanced diet will often result in poor skin, as a reflection of the unhealthy condition of other 'unseen' organs.

Below: Increase your circulation, develop a healthy glow and combat the effects of stress with a regular exercise programme.

Exercise Regular exercise helps the circulation and speeds the blood to the surface of the skin to help regenerate it. Not only do you look better immediately after exercise – having a healthy glow – but the long-term effects can be rejuvenating too. Exercise can also alleviate the negative effects of stress.

Stress This can have a drastic effect on the skin, causing blemishes, hives ('nettle-rash' lumps), loss of colour, and dark circles under the eyes. Having a constantly tense expression can also permanently line your face! Practise relaxing your facial muscles in order to avoid frowning or furrowing your brow when under stress.

Toxic Substances Nicotine, alcohol, caffeine and other drugs can be the skin's worst enemies. Smoking constricts the facial capillaries, allowing less blood, oxygen and nutrients to reach the surface of the skin and therefore making it look older. Alcohol and caffeine are diuretics that force moisture out of your system and dry out your skin. Some medication such as the Pill, can adversely affect your skin and make it more sensitive to other elements.

Analyzing Your Skin

With some understanding of the skin's structure and all the factors – controllable and uncontrollable – which can affect it, you now need to look closely at your own skin to assess the category it falls into. Start with an examination of the T-zone (forehead, nose and chin), then look at the cheek and eye areas. Take your time and consider all the following characteristics: texture, pore size, blemishes, fine lines, dry areas, oily areas

Your skin is probably one of four types: normal, normal-to-dry, normal-to-oily, sensitive

The T-zone comprises the forehead, nose and chin area.

Normal

The term 'normal skin' does not mean it is the most common! In fact, 'normal skin' is quite rare amongst adults and usually shares characteristics with dry or oily skin. Normal skin is most common amongst children and is characterized by:
- uniform texture and pigmentation
- skin areas clear, soft and supple
- no oily sheen or dry spots
- well-balanced secretion of sebum and moisture
- few or no blemishes
- small pore size
- few or no lines
- no difference between T-zone and cheek/eye areas

Normal-to-dry

On the T-zone:
- skin appears taut, fragile and dull
- forehead is prone to flaking and fine lines
- fine pores are visible
- blemishes are rare

On the cheek and eye areas:
- signs of flaking
- many fine lines around eyes and mouth

Normal-to-Dry Skin Needs:
- products that are non-drying
- products that will not clog pores
- a cleansing routine that does not strip the skin of natural oils
- to be kept moisturized at all times to prevent moisture loss
- a daytime sunscreen to avoid further signs of premature ageing

Normal-to-oily

On the T-zone:
- tends to have an oily sheen throughout the day
- enlarged pores visible especially on nose and chin
- blemishes are common

On the cheek and eye areas:
- skin appears soft and supple
- minimal fine lines around eyes and mouth

Normal-to-oily skin needs:
- non-greasy formulas that can help control oil and shine
- products that will not clog pores
- a cleansing routine without harsh scrubbing techniques which can over-stimulate the sebaceous glands
- cleansers that will keep the skin clean and free of oils
- sunscreen in a daytime moisturizer

Sensitive

This type of skin can be either dry or oily but is mainly defined as skin that is easily irritated.

Common characteristics are:
- stinging, itching, redness or blotchiness
- reacts to substances such as cosmetics, soaps, perfume, fabrics and chemicals such as sunscreens
- reacts to environmental irritants such as sun, wind and pollution

Sensitive skin needs:
- to be soothed and protected
- products that are mild and gentle
- products that are tested specifically for sensitive skin
- products that are carefully formulated to be effective without the inclusion of the most common irritants e.g. perfume, alcohol and lanolin

Techniques with Make-up

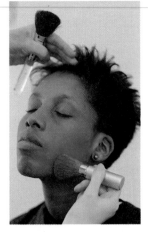

Make-up today should not be a mask. As with figure proportions, you need to highlight the good aspects of your face and bring out your best features and individuality. Problem areas can be played down with clever tricks of shade and light, but never attempt to alter your 'true self' dramatically as the results can be disastrous. Only cosmetic surgery can reduce a big nose to a small button one; so spend time playing up your eyes rather than hours trying to shade down your nose!

Base Products

The first step to successful make-up is to create a flawless background. Foundation and other base products should not add colour to the face but simply smooth out uneven skin tone and minimize imperfections while remaining as close to your natural skin tone as possible. Base products can also act as a barrier against the sun's rays and other harsh environmental factors mentioned earlier in this chapter. Most base products and moisturizers today contain sunscreens – select the Skin Protection Factor (SPF) which is best for your skin type, just as you would when buying a holiday sun-protection lotion.

Base controller: useful to correct and reduce unwanted colour in the skin tone. It is normally a green or lilac cream used to balance an excess of red or yellow in the skin. Choose green base controller to correct excess red in skin tone and lilac base controller to correct excess yellow.

How to apply:
- Dot on to forehead, nose, cheeks and chin before foundation
- Blend across forehead and downward and outward on to face with fingertips

- Blend evenly out to hairline and away at jawline, using light, swift strokes
- Leave to dry before applying foundation.

Concealer

Problem areas such as blemishes or dark circles under the eyes can be corrected by concealer, which comes in either cream or pencil format. Select a concealer a shade lighter than your skin tone to conceal dark areas and a shade that matches your skin tone to cover birthmarks or blemishes.

How to apply:
- Draw a line into the dark furrow in the inside corner of the eye
- Dot on any blemishes
- Use fingertips to gently pat the concealer until it is no longer visible
- Concealing can be done before or after applying foundation.

Foundations

These come in a variety of formulations to accommodate different skin types, weather and levels of coverage:

Liquid foundation (bottle) provides a light moisturizing coverage and is recommended for all skin types in all types of weather.

Crème foundation (jar) provides heavier coverage and is recommended for dry or mature skin. It also works well in drier, colder weather because its emollient-rich formula provides a moisture barrier against the drying environment.

Powder foundation (compact) is very versatile as it provides light, sheer coverage when used dry or heavier, matt coverage when used wet. Powder foundation can also be used to set other foundations or as a pressed powder for retouching. Unlike liquid or crème foundation, it does not require an application of loose powder on top. As it is often oil-free, it is also excellent for oily skin or for use when the weather is hot and humid.

How to apply liquid/crème foundation:
- Apply and blend with a very light touch, either with a sponge or your fingertips
- Dot foundation on to forehead, nose, cheeks and chin
- Blend foundation across forehead, toward the temples and out to the hairline
- Blend down nose, cheeks and chin, wrapping and blending away at jawline
- Always apply in a downward motion to minimize appearance of facial hair
- Make sure foundation is blended carefully, especially around nose and eyes
- Be sure to bring foundation up to the bottom lash line
- Foundation should not be visible on top of the skin. If it is, you may have applied too much – so remove excess with a clean sponge. Alternatively, the foundation is too dry for your skin type – so try a creamier formula
- Finish with loose powder (see opposite).

How to apply powder foundation:
- For lighter coverage, apply with a dry sponge, for heavier coverage, use a damp sponge
- Smooth the cosmetic sponge over the foundation
- Blend across forehead, towards temples and out to hairline
- Blend down nose, cheeks and chin, wrapping and blending away at jawline
- Use sparingly around eyes, as powder foundation can emphasize lines and wrinkles.

Loose Powder
To help your liquid or crème foundation last longer, set it by dusting lightly with loose powder.

How to apply:
- Use a light touch, as too much will cake in fine lines and look chalky and mask-like
- For a light application dip a powder brush into the powder, tap on the back of your hand or a tissue to remove excess, and dust lightly over the face
- For a heavier application, use a powder puff and work powder into foundation using a patting and rolling motion
- Brush away any excess with a powder brush.

Essential Tools

- Cosmetic sponge
- Powder brush/puff
- Blusher brush
- Eye shadow applicator (sponge tipped)
- Eye shadow brush
- Lipbrush

Colour Cosmetics

Now that you have prepared a flawless canvas, you can apply the colour cosmetics to enliven your features. It is the next stages – especially eyes and cheeks – which women can find most difficult, but follow these step-by-step guidelines and remember that practice makes perfect. No one has ever attained perfect results at their first attempt!

Left: Remember that practice makes perfect – no-one has ever attained perfect make-up results at the first attempt!

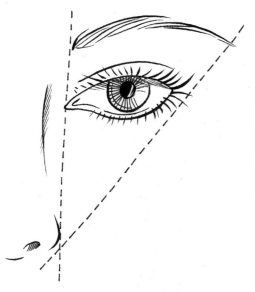

Eyebrows

The eyebrows frame the eyes and are one of the most expressive features of the face. Brows should be brushed and groomed first, after which shape and colour can be added with a pencil or powder. First use tweezers to remove any hairs that lie obviously outside the brow's natural shape. For the best shape, your brows should begin directly over the tear duct at the inner corner of the eye and rise in a gentle curve along the brow-bone. The highest point in the arch should be just about even with the outer edge of the eye's iris, tapering down and ending at the outside corner of the eye. To define the ideal length of the brow, line up a pencil perpendicular to the bridge of your nose and then at an angle across the outer edge of the eye (see left).

How to apply brow colour:
- Eyebrows should be a similar shade to your hair, so select a pencil/powder which complements your hair colour rather than contrasts with it – unless you want a dramatic effect!
- Use the natural brow shape as your guide, and enhance it without changing its fundamental shape
- The brow should be soft, with no sharp peaks: a pointed or very thin brow creates a harsh and/or surprised look!
- Always follow the direction of the hair growth and the natural curve of the brow, using light-handed, fine, feathery strokes rather than a harsh line.

Eye shadow

How and where eye shadow is used depends on the shape of the eyes and the desired effect. The following is a basic design using two shades of eye colour, which works for most eye shapes.

How to apply:
- Apply a light shade of eye shadow from lash line to brow
- Apply a compatible medium to darker shade of eye shadow in the crease, and blend up towards the outer edge towards the brow-bone
- Apply the medium shade also along the outer edge of the upper and lower lashes.

Eyeliner

Eyeliner goes in and out of fashion and can be used with eye shadow for further definition or alone for a more stark effect. Choose pencil or liquid – liquid is harsher and looks more dramatic.

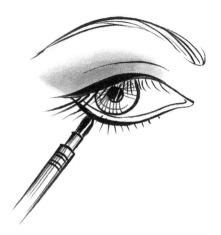

How to apply:

- Outline the outer edge of the eye only, unless you want to bring your eyes closer together
- Blend pencil liner with a foam-tip smudger or cotton bud to soften the line
- A thin line by the top lashes will make them appear thicker without the line being too visible
- For a minimal effect at the lower lashes, simply dot the colour between lashes
- If you have dark shadows under your eyes, don't line the lower lashes as this can emphasize the shadows.

Mascara

Whether you are blessed with long, dark eyelashes or need to enhance and dramatize light, sparse or short lashes, mascara can make your eyelashes look longer, fuller and more luxurious.

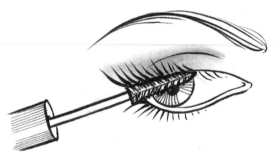

How to apply:

- Tilt your head forward and apply mascara to the lower lashes first, using downward rotating strokes
- Tilt your head backwards to apply mascara to the upper lashes
- Allow to dry, then apply a second coat if necessary.

Blusher

The idea of blusher is to give a subtle, natural glow of colour while adding contour to your face. You can change your blusher to co-ordinate with your clothing or keep to one constant neutral shade, but it should always appear as a natural, light flush of colour on the cheeks – not a harsh streak or round blob!

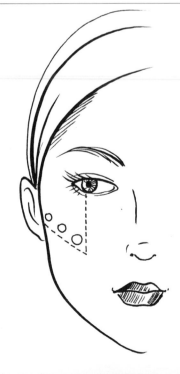

How to apply:

- When using powder blusher remove excess colour from the brush by patting it on the back of your hand or a tissue
- Locate your cheekbone and apply the blusher directly on top, blending up towards the top of the ear and well into the hairline
- Blusher should not be placed any lower than the nose and no further in than under the pupil of the eye (see right)
- Use a cotton ball or brush dipped in loose powder to blend the edges of the blusher into the surrounding skin. This will also stop your blusher from fading during the day
- If you are not wearing powder, a crème blusher (or lipstick) will give a better effect than powder blusher.

Lip colour

Lipstick is that all-important final touch that pulls a total look together. Many women depend on lipstick more than any other cosmetic to add brightness and to freshen up their appearance. Often, lipstick is the last thing checked before going out and the first thing renewed in a spare moment! Plus, with an easy change of lipstick you can alter your total look in just a minute or two. Always use a lip-liner, in the same shade as your lipstick or as close a match as possible, to define the shape of your mouth and prevent feathering.

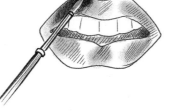

How to apply:

- Place two dots of lip-liner on the upper lip, on the area called the 'Cupid's bow'
- Directly below, place two more dots on the lower lip
- Then join the dots, starting from the upper lip and working down and around
- Use a lip brush to apply lipstick within and on the line created by the lip-liner
- Blot with a tissue to remove excess lipstick
- Dust with powder for a matt finish or gloss for shine.

Nails

Your nails can speak volumes about you! Often in interviews a note is taken of the state of two things: shoes and nails. Nice nails help to give a positive impression of health, attitude and self-esteem. It is not necessary to match your nail and lip colours, but your nail colour should blend with cosmetic and wardrobe shades if you wish to achieve a co-ordinated look.

Perfect Manicure Routine

- Remove all traces of old nail colour with nail varnish remover
- Shape nails with the coarse side of an emery board, stroking from the side towards the centre of the nail only. Never saw back and forth
- Finish with the fine side of the emery board. Nails squared at the tip and slightly rounded at the corners are most attractive and remain stronger than a tapered shape
- Soak hands in warm water or wash them before applying polish, to ensure adhesion

Remove old polish

Soak in water

Shape with emery board

Apply polishes

- Apply a base coat again to help nail colour adhere. If your nails are fragile and tend to split, keep them short and apply base coat twice. Allow enough time for each coat to dry before continuing your manicure
- Apply the nail colour in three strokes: one down the centre of the nail and one down each side. Wait about five minutes or until nails feel dry to the touch (time varies according to temperature)
- Apply a second coat. It is always better to apply two thin coats of polish than one thick layer. Let second coat dry thoroughly.
- Apply a top coat to protect both nails and colour. Let dry.

Evening glamour

More dramatic make-up can be applied in the evening. Brows can be more defined, eye colour more expressive and lip colour stronger. Evening allows you to experiment and have fun!

■ Foundation can be heavier and more matt. Use either powder foundation applied with a wet sponge, or crème foundation. Set with loose powder.

■ Brows can be one-half to one shade darker than they are naturally. Pencil-in a heavier arched shape. Keep the brow symmetrical and follow the natural shape.

Above and left: Enhance your 'everyday' look for the evening with darker eye shadow, shiny highlighter, liquid eyeliner, glossy lips and an up-pinned hairstyle.

■ Apply a darker-than-usual shade of eye shadow in a line in the crease of the eye. This will make the eyelid look larger.

■ Blend a shiny eye shadow over the brow-bone. This will make the structure of the brow-bone stronger. A dab of the shiny shadow can also be put in the centre of the eyelid.

■ Apply liquid liner along upper lashes. Start at the inner corner of the eye with a thin line, creating a thicker line along the iris. Extend the line diagonally upward past the outer corner of the eye.

■ Line lower lashes with a subtly coloured eye pencil and blend.

■ Apply two coats of mascara to upper and lower lashes – coloured can be fun!

■ Apply a medium to dark shade of powder blusher under the cheekbone. Apply a lighter shade over the cheekbone and on to the ball of the cheek. Blend up and out towards hairline.

■ Dab lip gloss (or Vaseline) onto the centre of your bottom lip over your lipstick.

Cosmetic tips for mature skin

As we get older our colouring fades as melanin and carotene levels reduce and pigments are thus lost from the hair, eyes and skin. The blood supply to the skin lessens, so the 'rosy' look of youth is also lost, and skin-cell renewal reduces leaving the skin thicker and more 'opaque'. Cosmetics can be very useful, therefore, to help older women put some colour back into their appearance – this automatically gives a younger, healthier look. This is particularly important if your Colour Direction is Cool, the colour pattern containing the least pigment.

Here are some flattering make-up tips for the mature woman at any time:

Above: Matt eye shadow, soft eye pencil, light-reflecting foundation, and 'lifting' blush and lip colours are most flattering for the mature woman.

- Use concealer pencil to cover dark circles and blemishes such as brown pigmentation or liver spots.
- Use liquid foundation for light coverage and crème foundation for extra moisturizing coverage. Avoid compact foundation. Light-reflecting foundation is very flattering, as it reduces the effect of lines.
- Because skin tone and colour fade with age, be sure to check your foundation colour. It may need to change to give a boost to your skin tone. Review your foundation colour every three or four years.
- Use powder sparingly! If you apply it too heavily, lines and wrinkles will be accentuated. Keep it to nose, cheeks and chin only. Light reflecting powder is also good.
- Shape the brows and fill in any sparse areas with eye pencil or powder. Avoid using black, because it can be too harsh.
- Use matt eye shadow because frosted tends to emphasize crèpiness on drier, ageing skin.
- Don't apply colour under the lower lashes because it can appear darker and give your skin a tired, washed-out look.
- Use soft eye pencil (not liquid eyeliner) to line the top lashes and blend it in. Avoid very dark colours.

Above: Remember to lower the position of your blusher slightly if you wear glasses and balance the strength of your lipstick to the strength of your frame.

- Apply two light coats of mascara. Choose brown or grey because black can be too harsh, unless your colouring is Deep.
- As we age the skin sags, resulting in loss of bone definition. This condition can be helped by the correct application of blusher to give a lift to the cheeks and jawline.
- To prevent lipstick from feathering or bleeding, apply foundation and powder to your lips first.

Cosmetic tips for women who wear glasses

The effect of make-up varies according to the type of glasses worn. Lenses for near-sighted people make their eyes appear smaller, so their make-up needs to enlarge the eyes. It may even be necessary to try stronger make-up. Lenses for far-sighted people, however, magnify the eyes, so their make-up should not be too strong – take special care to avoid 'globby' mascara!

- Always apply make-up to the whole face. Don't ignore the lips or cheeks, or you will create an imbalance.
- If your eyesight makes applying make-up difficult, try using a magnifying mirror or special make-up glasses with individual tip-down lenses.
- Eye colour can be a little deeper in shade than usual, as glasses slightly lighten the effect of the colour of eye shadow.
- Eye colours should complement the shade of the frames unless a contrast is desired.
- Lower the position of your blusher a little if it is covered by the arms of the glasses.
- If the frames are a strong colour, your face should be balanced with a strong lipstick for a harmonious look.

6 Chapter

Wardrobe Directions

Y ou will be pleased to know that the analysis of your face, figure, wobbly bits, colouring and so on is completely finished. All we need to do now is pool that information and start to plan your perfect future wardrobe. You probably have a few ideas by now of items that you would like to buy, but before you make any additions to your wardrobe it's useful to do a little pruning – to clear out the dead wood and to make space for your new clothes and accessories.

Weeding Is Worthwhile

When was the last time you made a really ruthless attack on your clothes mountain? Last year? Last time you moved house? Last century? Yes, now that's entirely possible! The problem is that most women are hoarders. The squirrel instinct does not just apply to clothes, however – cosmetics, shoes, handbags, jewellery and even ancient pairs of tights are all crammed into drawers and cupboards awaiting that magical day when they just might be needed again. Perhaps you'll slim into them next year – oh, no you won't! Or perhaps they'll come back into fashion – but not in that old fabric! Excuses for keeping old clothes are many and varied, but the real reason, deep down inside, is usually the fact that they have cost hard-earned money and it seems wasteful to ditch them.

You therefore need to see wardrobe weeding as having positive benefits, rather than dwelling on negative, guilty feelings. Having a planned, organized wardrobe is eventually going to save you time and money – it won't happen overnight, but the long-term effects are worthwhile. Getting rid of old belongings can be quite therapeutic – like a cleansing ritual which heralds a new beginning or phase of your life! Some of the good items can be sold to 'Nearly New' or 'Designer Seconds' shops and the money put towards some new purchases. Lesser items can be given to charity shops – far better that they are used by someone who needs them rather than collecting dust, hanging unworn in your wardrobe.

Above: Wouldn't you love a wardrobe which is worn on a fairly regular basis and provides outfits for all occasions?

When I mention in presentations that women wear 20 per cent of their clothing 80 per cent of the time, I see most of the audience nod in agreement. Nearly all women identify with this but don't know what to do to rectify the situation. The majority would dearly love a wardrobe which not only suits them perfectly but is worn on a fairly regular basis and provides outfits for all occasions. Can this miracle wardrobe be achieved? Yes, if you take the time to work out your own individual needs.

Analyzing Your Lifestyle

Think back over the last three or four months (look at your diary if necessary) and try to work out roughly what proportion of your time is spent on different types of activities – working, socializing, leisure and so on. Draw yourself a pie-chart like the examples shown and divide it into slices which represent as closely as possible the percentage of time you spend on those activities each week. Obviously this will differ from one woman to the next – a busy executive will spend maybe half her time in the office and perhaps a further quarter on socializing, leaving only perhaps 12½ per cent for sport/active time and 12½ per cent for rest and leisure activities. A young mother with children, however, may spend 50 per cent of her time working in the home, 25 per cent on leisure activities, 10 per cent on sport/active and 15 per cent on socializing.

Not only do lifestyles differ from individual to individual, but your own lifestyle will change as you enter and leave different stages of your life. The pie-charts (left) could, in fact, belong to the same woman. Chart A could be a woman in her twenties, unmarried, establishing a career and socializing a great deal with friends and colleagues. Chart B could be the same woman in her thirties after she has married and chosen to stay at home to look after young children – home and leisure have increased, while sport and socializing have decreased. The most important change of all, however, is that 50 per cent of the wardrobe of her twenties needed to be 'executive wear', whereas in her thirties it

Working executive lifestyle

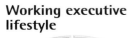

socializing   sport/active   leisure

Mother-at-home lifestyle

needs to be 50 per cent 'home wear' – and baby-proof! If our hypothetical woman had decided to work part- or full-time after having her children, another slice would be needed in the pie to reflect the need for office wear.

In other words, as your lifestyle changes, your wardrobe needs to reflect those changes in the type of clothing, accessories, shoes and so on that you buy. Unfortunately we all tend to be creatures of habit, and just as we can get stuck in the rut of buying the same styles, colours and cosmetics, we can also get stuck in the rut of buying a certain type of clothing for a person that we no longer are – or perhaps never were!

Below: Make sure you have the right proportion of clothes to suit the life you lead – work out your percentages for work, leisure and socializing.

Once you have completed your pie-chart, you should have a rough idea of the percentage of clothes you need within each category. If, for example, most of your waking time is spent at work but you have far more leisure/weekend/casual clothes than work-wear, you know where your money should be spent. Conversely, if you spend most time at home but have a wardrobe full of suits and cocktail dresses from a past life, change your shopping habits.

You need to look and feel good for the majority of the time, not just when you 'go out'; and this means spending the most money on the clothes you wear most often. For instance, invest in

several good outfits for work, if that's how you are dressed most often, rather than wearing the same one or two outfits over and over again which will only result in that familiar 'nothing to wear' syndrome! Conversely it is pointless (and depressing) to spend lots of money on an outfit for a wedding or Christmas and then hardly wear it while you spend the rest of your time in the same old (cheaper) clothes. Buy something that is good quality but relatively simple in style that can be dressed up with jewellery and a hat for the wedding or down for less formal occasions afterwards.

The real cost of an item is its price divided by the number of times you wear it. If 80 per cent or more of the clothes in your wardrobe hardly ever get worn (or perhaps have never been worn at all) they have really been a waste of money. In a truly effective wardrobe most pieces are worn on a regular basis, with only a few items reserved for special occasions.

Biting the Bullet!

Time to get all your clothes out of the wardrobes, drawers, boxes, bin-bags and so on and pile them on your bed – if they'll fit. If you have far too many clothes, you may need to take a weekend to do this exercise and refill the bed several times! Divide the items into three piles:

1. Clothes worn frequently
2. Clothes worn sometimes
3. Clothes not worn for a year or more

Pile No. 1: Clothes Worn Frequently

These can go back into the wardrobe as you probably like and feel comfortable in all these garments – it is likely they suit your shape, colouring and so forth. Also, they will tend to be quite recent purchases and therefore fashionable.

Pile No. 2: Clothes Worn Sometimes

These probably consist of 'occasional' wear (parties, weddings, holidays), or items which don't quite fit into your lifestyle. These can go back too, but you may need to buy some pieces to go with them to make them more versatile. They could be the starting point of some new, versatile 'capsules', which are explained later in this chapter.

Pile No. 3: Clothes Not Worn for a Year or More

You have to be ruthless with these. Although it is probably the biggest heap, it has to go! If you can't bear to get rid of these clothes altogether, put them away in bin-bags somewhere other than your bedroom and forget about them. If it's another year before you go back to them, they will be much easier to get rid of as out of sight is out of mind. The chances are that these clothes don't fit you; are old-fashioned; are wrong for your shape or colouring; or belong to a past life you used to lead but don't now.

Underwear

I did say we were going to be thorough, so the underwear drawer must not be forgotten either in this ruthless pruning exercise. It would be a shame to ruin new clothes – bought in your best styles and colours – with old, saggy undies beneath. Well-fitting underwear can also be extremely slimming as it can smooth out lumps and bumps, lift and separate where needed, and even hold in an extra inch or two if necessary. As there are only seven days in a week, it isn't necessary to have twenty pairs of bras and pants – usually several years old and in varying shades of grey!

Bras
Get rid of:
- any which dig heavily into your shoulders – you need broader shoulder straps
- any which cause 'arm-pit cleavage' or 'overflowing' cups – you need a bigger cup size (AA, A, B, C, D, DD, etc.)
- any which ride up at the back – you need a smaller band size (32, 34, 36, 38 etc.)
- any which have lost their shape, elasticity or underwires

If you haven't been measured recently for a new bra, visit your nearest department store for some expert advice.

Briefs
Get rid of:
- any which ride up when you move – you need more back coverage
- any which dig into your flesh on the hips – you need wider side coverage
- any which cause your stomach to bulge over the top elastic – you need a higher waistline and perhaps a tummy control panel
- any which have lost their shape, colour or elasticity

Hosiery
This is usually the most seriously overcrowded drawer (or drawers) of all. Get rid of:
- any which are snagged, laddered or holed
- any which are poor-fitting and uncomfortable
- any in hideous colours from several seasons (or years) ago
- any in glossy, patterned or too-light colours unless your legs are very slim

Why, when tights cost about the same as a bunch of flowers, do we hang on to them for several years? Would you keep a dead bunch of flowers in a vase for so long?

Core Items

Jewellery

Get rid of:

- any pieces which are the wrong scale for your body
- any pieces which are old-fashioned and outdated
- any earrings and necklaces which have the wrong lines for your facial features
- any which are broken/scratched or generally tatty

Leather Accessories

Get rid of:

- any shoes and bags which are the wrong scale for your body size
- any leather goods which are scuffed, scratched or tatty
- any belts which are too narrow or too wide for your figure
- any shoes and bags which are old-fashioned – nothing spoils a current outfit more than outdated shoes and bags

Stop the Gaps

With your pie-chart highlighting your 'needy' wardrobe zones and with a little space now cleared to incorporate some new buys, it is time to plan your future shopping trips and make lists of suggested presents from friends or family for your birthday, Christmas or anniversary. There are some items now regarded as wardrobe classics which all women can wear regardless of their age or lifestyle. If you are missing any of the following six 'core' items, put some at the top of your list and buy the best that you can in terms of fabric and cut. The definition of a classic is a garment whose colour, fabric and style remain 'outside' fashion trends and fads and therefore never become outdated.

The LBD (little black dress): so much an accepted part of the fashion scene now that it is often simply referred to by its initials! Yes, it is a cliché – but every wardrobe needs one and it is ideal for 'black-tie' functions when your man is in his dinner jacket. Black, as everyone knows, is the most slimming of colours as long as the fabric is matt. Personalize it with your favourite accessories, shoes and make-up for the impact you desire!

Navy Blazer: for effortless continental chic, a good blazer cannot be beaten. For a casual look, wear it with jeans and a T-shirt; on semi-casual days team it with a sweater and classic trousers; and with a silk blouse and tailored skirt it can take you to the smartest of occasions. A blazer can even be invaluable for evenings – with elegant palazzo pants, a camisole top and gold jewellery to echo the blazer buttons.

White or ivory shirt: in my experience, for many people pure white is the most difficult colour to wear next to the face. If your colouring is very Deep or Bright (see Chapter 4) a pure white shirt or blouse can look stunning, but for lighter or more muted colour patterns ivory or oyster white will be kinder to the complexion. Warm-toned, freckled skins, particularly with red hair, will always look best with cream. Keep the shirt as simple in design as possible so that it could even be worn with jeans on casual occasions. Some stunning jewellery will transform it for parties.

Cotton knitwear: much more versatile than chunky, woollen knitwear as it will keep you snug and warm in the winter, layered with shirts, blouses and jackets, while keeping your skin cool and itch-free in the summer. A really good investment would be a sweater-set comprising a sleeveless or short-sleeved sweater with matching cardigan. In the hot summer months wear the sweater alone with shorts or a skirt, keeping the cardigan at hand to slip on for cooler evenings. In the winter, wear the sweater as a layering piece under a shirt with the cardigan on top teamed with jacket and trousers.

Soft Trouser Suit: a really versatile all-year-round outfit – especially if it is in a neutral colour. Look for lightweight, crease-resistant fabrics, elasticated or drawstring waists, side-splits in jackets and collarless styles for extreme comfort and ease. Worn with a T-shirt and flat shoes, soft trouser-suits are ideal for travelling – especially on planes. In winter they can be worn with the cotton sweater of your twin-set and in summer a silky camisole beneath the jacket looks perfect – especially for evening.

Denim: if you feel that your bottom is a little too wide for all the horizontal lines on the back of denim jeans, simply wear a shirt, sweater or blazer over the top for a relaxed and easy style. Jeans used to be cut only in a 'straight' style as they were originally a garment for men. Today, however, there are shapes of jeans to suit all women's figures, and advances in fibre technologies have produced denims which are softer, stretch-ier and far more comfortable. Worn with T-shirts and plimsolls in summer, and with jackets, boots or loafers in winter, jeans have stayed the test of time although other casual trousers, such as chinos, are fast gaining in popularity. If you really dislike denim, chinos are an excellent alternative as they can, in fact, be more flattering because they have much less detail. If you dislike trousers altogether, a denim dress is an alternative classic. A sleeveless, button-fronted style is most versatile, but

Above: Soft trouser suits, cotton twin-sets, Little Black Dresses and classic denim jeans have all become wardrobe basics.

choose a straighter or more fitted style if it suits your body shape better. In winter team it with a sweater, tights and boots, while in summer its only essential accessories are flat leather sandals and some casual jewellery. For cooler summer days a cotton T-shirt can be layered beneath, or knot your crisp white shirt on top.

Versatile Capsules

Once the 'core' classics have been added, you need to begin building capsules each season to ring the changes with your outfits and obtain real value for money. A capsule is simply a collection of garments based around a few colours which will mix and match into dozens of different outfits. A capsule of just twelve garments, for example, can provide over sixty outfits – so although you may have fewer clothes in your wardrobe, you will have ten times the amount of outfits. The 'nothing to wear' syndrome will be gone forever!

If you spend a great deal of time at home, don't think of building capsules as being 'too smart' for your lifestyle. 'A suit' simply means a jacket and bottom which match – the fabric could even be denim. The trousers in your capsule could be chinos and the three tops could all be T-shirts, sweatshirts or bodies, if your lifestyle does not require anything more dressy. In the summer your two-piece dress, for example, could be a sarong skirt with matching shirt. Your one-piece dress could be anything from a knitted sweater dress to a spaghetti-strapped slip dress. Interpret the capsule idea to suit your age, lifestyle, personality and budget.

Start to build capsules each season for the kind of life you lead. A working woman may need eventually to have several 'smart' capsules but only one leisure one; a student/young mum may need several leisure capsules and only one smarter one.

Sample Capsule for Light Colouring

A and B – jacket and skirt in neutral colour (e.g. navy)
C and D – jacket and skirt in toning colour (e.g. taupe)
E – daytime shirt (eg pale-blue cotton)
F – casual T-shirt/body (e.g. cream stretch jersey)
G – Evening blouse (e.g. lilac satin)
H – Pair of trousers (e.g. navy to match A and B)
I and J – Two-piece dress (e.g. navy/lilac/cream pattern)
K – Knit-top (e.g. navy or cream)
L – Cardigan – (e.g. navy or cream)

From a typical capsule the following combinations are possible:

1. I-J-L	21. J-F-L	41. F-K-D
2. I-J-K	22. J-F-K	42. F-K-H
3. I-J-A	23. J-G-L	43. F-A-B
4. I-J-C	24. J-G-K	44. F-C-D
5. I-L-B	25. J.E.A	45 F-C-H
6. I-L-D	26. J-E-C	46. F-A-H
7. I-A-B	27. J-F-A	47. G-L-B
8. I-A-D	28. J-F-C	48. G-L-D
9. I-A-H	29. J-G-A	49. G-L-H
10. I-C-D	30. J-G-C	50. G-L-H
11. I-C-H	31. E-A-B	51. G-A-D
12. I-L-H	32. E-C-D	52. G-B-C
13. I-B-L	33. E-B-C	53. G-K-H
14. I-K-B	34. E-L-B	54. G-C-H
15. I-K-D	35. E-L-D	55. G-A-H
16. I-K-H	36. E-L-H	56. G-K-D
17. E-J	37. E-K-D	57. G-H
18. F-J	38. F-L-B	58. E-K-H
19. G-J	39. F-L-D	59. E-A-H
20. J-E-L	40. F-L-H	60. E-C-H

Left: This outfit is a typical capsule combination – A (suit jacket) + H (matching trousers) + G (satin blouse) = Success!

Every woman will benefit from putting together a capsule for summer holidays. Choose clothes that are lightweight and not bulky (for air travel) and crease resistant but cool. If you attend lots of social functions you may want to build a capsule of co-ordinating evening separates which is much more versatile and cost-effective than a range of 'unconnected' evening dresses.

Although there are over sixty outfits listed left you can make even more. Wearing two of the tops together (for instance a shirt over a T-shirt/body) with the different jackets and bottoms gives additional possibilities. Don't forget that you also have your 'core' pieces which can be integrated into the plan – the coloured jacket over the black dress, the sweater under the blazer and so on. The possibilities become endless and, as you add new capsules each season, they will also soon all begin to mix together.

Capsules, therefore, make life incredibly easy and can be put together for any lifestyle. Obviously they are a great boon to working women, particularly those who travel frequently. One capsule, plus a variety of accessories, will easily see a busy working woman through a one-week business trip.

Also, each capsule only needs three pairs of shoes, especially for holidays. Choose in neutral colours to take you to all occasions
- a flat pair (e.g. loafers) for casual
- a medium heel (e.g. court shoes) for day
- a higher heel (e.g. slingback sandals) for evening

The following pages show examples of capsules for different body shapes with some slight variations in content for different seasons.

Straight Figure Direction: Winter Wardrobe

Check coat with fur
collar and cuffs

Herringbone jacket

Long straight blouse

Straight sweater with embroidery
detail

Straight-leg herringbone trousers

Straight evening dress with
pointed hem detail

Pinstripe coat dress

Straight tweed jacket

Gilet

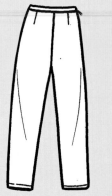

Casual trousers with side zip

Side-split tweed skirt   High closure tweed waistcoat

Straight Figure Direction: Summer Wardrobe

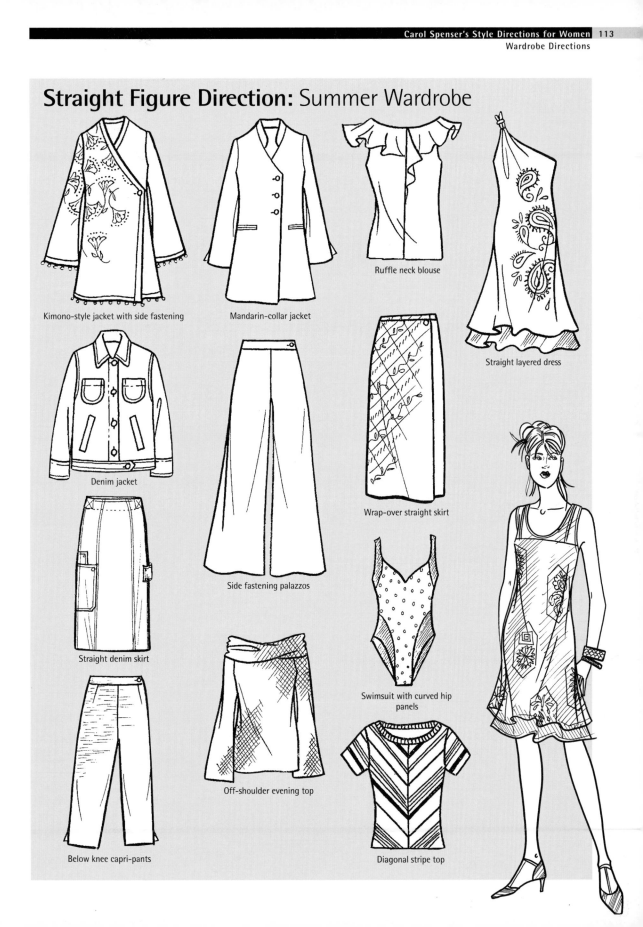

Kimono-style jacket with side fastening

Mandarin-collar jacket

Ruffle neck blouse

Straight layered dress

Denim jacket

Side fastening palazzos

Wrap-over straight skirt

Straight denim skirt

Swimsuit with curved hip panels

Off-shoulder evening top

Below knee capri-pants

Diagonal stripe top

Tapered Figure Direction: Winter Wardrobe

Princess-style coat

Semi-fitted pinstripe jacket

Tapered shirt with French cuffs

Side fastening
oriental-style tunic

Tapered leg pinstripe
trousers

Semi-fitted pinstripe waistcoat

Wide palazzo pants

Semi-fitted check jacket

Evening-dress
with dipped hemline

Tweed dress with
lace hem detail

Long, panelled check skirt

Cable-knit cardigan with
fur collar and cuffs

Tapered Figure Direction: Summer Wardrobe

Two-button semi-fitted jacket

Princess-line, soft jacket

Ribbed cotton knit

Empire-style floaty dress

No-waistband, drape skirt

Waistcoat evening top

Darted palazzo pants

Drawstring-hem pants

Semi-fitted check blouse

Side-tie, wrap-over skirt

Thin-waistband capri-pants

Empire-style check swimsuit

Curved Figure Direction: Winter Wardrobe

Bathrobe style coat with velvet collar and cuffs

Belted tweed jacket

Centre-fastening, fitted jacket

Fitted blouse with tied collar and cuffs

A-line tweed skirt

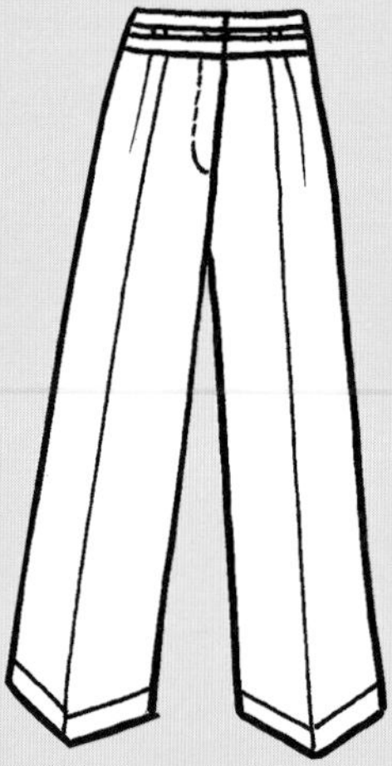

Brocade evening waistcoat

High-waisted wide trousers

Wrap-over ethnic style cardigan

Tie-back blouse with flared cuffs

Wrap-style, belted dress

Side-split evening dress with wide sash

Low-waisted casual trousers

Curved Figure Direction: Summer Wardrobe

Sash-belted jacket

Tie-side floral blouse

Lingerie-style sweater

Belted apron-dress

Wide waistband skirt

Darted, wrap-over skirt

High-waisted slim trousers

Drawstring-waist shorts

Lacey vest-top

Roll-down top and bottom bikini

Halter-neck evening top

Tie-waisted floral palazzos

Fuller Figure Direction: Winter Wardrobe

Coat with fur collar and cuffs

Jacket with vertical pockets

Long loose tunic

Long-line cardigan

Straight single breasted jacket

Side fastening trousers

Jersey day dress

Long-line sweater

Straight wrap-over skirt

Oriental Evening dress

Long gillet

Loose over-shirt

Fuller Figure Direction: Summer Wardrobe

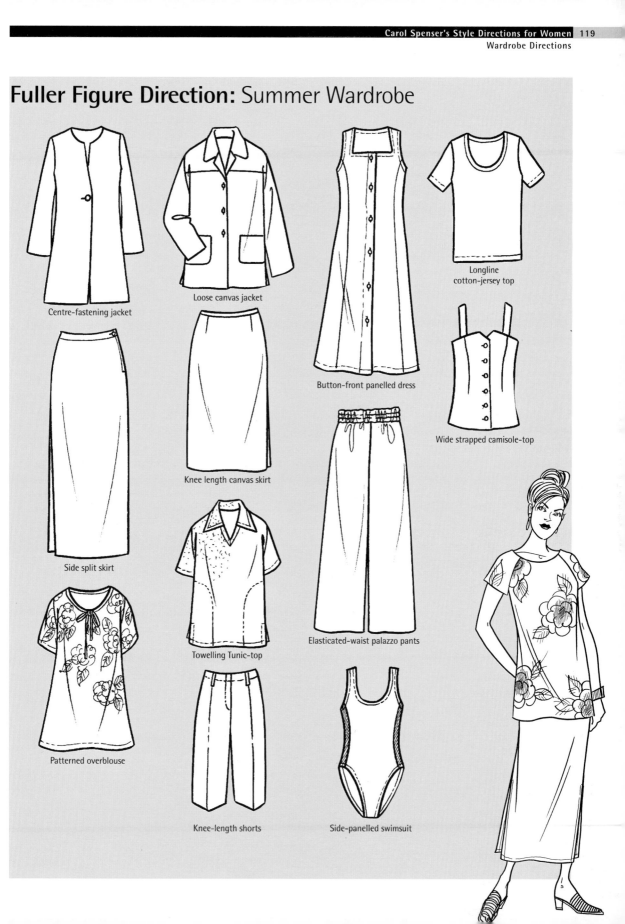

Centre-fastening jacket

Loose canvas jacket

Button-front panelled dress

Longline cotton-jersey top

Side split skirt

Knee length canvas skirt

Wide strapped camisole-top

Elasticated-waist palazzo pants

Towelling Tunic-top

Patterned overblouse

Knee-length shorts

Side-panelled swimsuit

Selective Shopping

Once you start wardrobe planning, shopping trips can become purposeful and planned rather than haphazard and often fruitless. Instead of going out to buy 'something' (you're not really sure what), make a list of the items your wardrobe actually needs. Perhaps some of the core items; maybe a second suit to mix 'n' match with another one; an evening top to dress up a black skirt; or a polo-neck sweater to dress down some velvet trousers. You might not find all these things on one trip, or even be able to afford all the things on one trip; but, armed with a list, you are bound to find at least one good purchase to tick off on the list. If, by chance, you do have an unsuccessful day, still treat yourself to a few inexpensive accessories – a new scarf, a necklace or a bag – to update the outfits at home. Keep a list of your wardrobe 'must haves' in your purse or pinned inside your wardrobe door – it's very satisfying to tick off the items over the months.

Above: Treat youself to a scarf or other accessory if your shopping trip is unsuccessful!

It is always advisable to shop for major purchases such as coats, jackets, skirts and trousers at the beginning of the season, when a wide choice of styles, colours and sizes is available. If you find one particular shop whose style, fit and colours you really like, it may be worth taking one of their customer account cards so that you can make major purchases at the beginning of the season and spread the cost over several months. There is nothing worse than buying a jacket and skirt and returning for the trousers next month, only to discover that they have sold out or have only size 8s remaining! Often you will be invited to preview evenings at the beginning of each season and receive advance information of sales and special promotions. Also, let the staff know the kinds of items you are looking for so that they can telephone you when new stock arrives. Stores with a good 'Personal Shopping' department should be trained in all aspects of style, proportions, colour and wardrobe planning.

Wardrobe Revelations

The final aspect of wardrobe planning relates to the piece of furniture itself and how you arrange your clothes within it. Most women's wardrobes tend to be a hotchpotch of different garments hung randomly, often with several garments on one hanger. Now that you have cleared a little space, invest in some new hangers (get rid of all the wire ones) and hang all your garments by category. You probably already do this with drawers – a jumper drawer, an underwear drawer, a T-shirt drawer – but for some reason, most of us don't extend this discipline to our wardrobe.

If you hang all your jackets together, all your skirts together, all your trousers together, all your shirts/blouses together and so on, you will begin to see potential combinations for outfits that you had never considered. When a suit is put on a hanger as a suit, that is the way it is usually worn. Think of three different ways to wear everything you have by combining items or dressing them up or down with different accessories or shoes. And, finally, never again utter those words, 'I've nothing to wear'.

Above: Trousers together, blouses together, dresses together, jackets together... get organized!

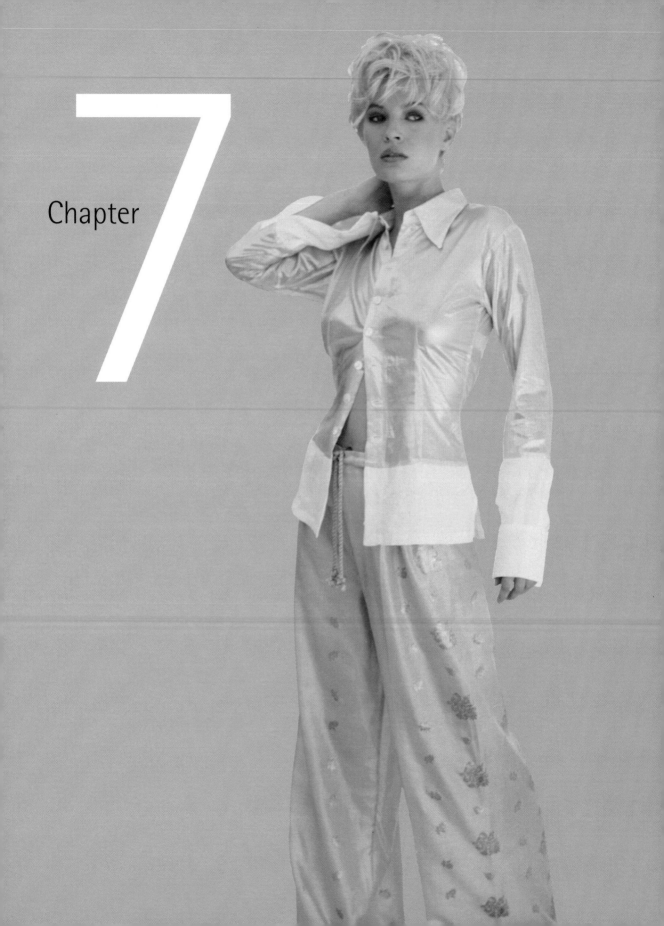

Chapter

7

Fashion Directions

Ahigh proportion of my heavy mailbag is concerned with that elusive topic, fashion. It seems that the crazy world it encompasses is quite bewildering to lots of women, who feel it is only for teenagers or extroverts who live in big cities! At the same time they find the subject intriguing and would actually like to incorporate it more into their lives if only they knew something about it and understood how to adapt it to their age and personality.

The most common questions are these. Where on earth do fashion trends come from? How can you personalize fashion for yourself? At what age should you stop following fashion? Two particular items also seem to cause enormous problems for women and prompt two more frequently asked questions. How do you manage to look good with not much on – say a swimsuit? And what is the secret to not looking stupid in a hat? So for all those women out there who ponder these questions time and time again, here at last are the answers!

Where Do Fashion Trends Come From?

It may often seem that fashion originates from outer space, but in reality it is just a reflection of what is happening here on our own planet at any given time. Social trends, political events, economic factors and even the practical developments in yarn manufacture all have an effect on the clothes which end up on the catwalk, in the shops and eventually in our wardrobes.

Fashion designers, being creative people, are very much in tune with the mood of the time, which is then reflected in the clothing they produce. Think of women's fashions during the Second World War – sober times called for sober colours; fabric was in short supply, so silhouettes were narrow; women were doing men's jobs, so styles were quite masculine. Contrast that with the period immediately following the war – new hope for the future was reflected in brighter colours; fabric became plentiful again and resulted in wide, full skirts and dresses; women returned to being 'homemakers and child-bearers', so styles became extremely feminine.

Above: Styles seen on the catwalks or in fashion magazines can often look ridiculous and completely unwearable – do not dismiss them but search for the clues of the season's new looks.

Right: The military look may be exaggerated on the catwalk but will find its way onto the High Street in a much more diluted form.

As advances in communication shrink our planet into one global village, fashion itself is becoming increasingly global with each season's trends, colours and styles now being seen all over the world. After the outrageous 'youth culture' fashions of the 1960s, the romantic 'peace and love' fashions of the 1970s and the aggressive 'self-interested' fashions of the 1980s, we enter the new millennium seeing trends shifting towards hope and spirituality (the so-called 'New Age') with the emphasis on comfortable styles, understatement and individuality.

How Do You Personalize Fashion?

The styles seen on catwalks or in the latest magazines can often look ridiculous and completely unwearable by most women. Do not, however, dismiss these fashions completely and decide that fashion is no longer for you. Remember that the designers are competing madly for publicity and the more outrageous the outfit, the more publicity they receive. Simply look for the clues in the catwalk pictures – the colours, fabrics, key pieces, accessories and so on – and decide to what extent you want to incorporate these into your own look, dependent on your 'fashion-personality'. Study the descriptions overleaf and tick the box

which most describes your preferred style or the style you want to be:

- ❑ **Trendy** – latest look, extreme and exaggerated
- ❑ **Contemporary** – current look but not extreme
- ❑ **Classic** – timeless look which never changes

Trendy very often applies to the teens and twenties age-group, who feel it is more important to wear what fashion or their friends dictate rather than what suits them personally. Older people who continue to dress in this way are often in artistic careers or have extremely extrovert personalities. Trendy clothes can be very 'body-conscious' and difficult for older or fuller-figured women to wear.

Contemporary – most women from their late twenties onwards would like to develop a contemporary style, but some find it difficult to do so. They may have been trendy when younger, but become afraid of the mutton-dressed-as-lamb image as they get older and therefore opt for a classic look. A contemporary look keeps you looking and feeling younger and is quite easy to achieve whatever your age or size.

Classic is a very 'safe' way of dressing, often favoured by older or fuller-figured women who feel afraid to follow fashion or simply have no interest in the latest looks. Classic does not have to be boring, however. Simply by using fashionable accessories, a 'currently classic' look can be achieved which prevents a classic outfit from looking old-fashioned.

Trends today can permeate all areas of fashion from babywear (top left) to childrenswear (bottom left) to classic and contemporary womenswear (above) – and even houseware (below).

Fashion Seasons

Every year there are two fashion seasons: spring/summer and autumn/winter. Each season has several themes reflecting current moods, and each theme will have trendy, contemporary and more classic items within it for you to choose from. Each theme also has a wide range of accessories to complete the look or simply to wear with your existing wardrobe.

At the time of writing there is a trend for animal print designs which has arisen out of the animal rights movement's lobbying to ban real fur in fashion, followed by the huge technological advances in the manufacture of realistic fake fur. This trend has permeated almost every fashion item: coats, jackets, skirts, trousers, hats, bags, belts, boots and even jewellery (I am the proud owner of a pair of leopard-print earrings!). The catwalk, of course, took this theme to extremes with 'lion's-mane' hairstyles and 'tiger-face' make-up. The woman who prefers the trendsetting look may go for a full-length, zebra-striped, fake fur coat; the contemporary woman may choose a suit with animal-print collar and cuffs; and the classic woman needs only a fake fur-trimmed hat, scarf, bag or gloves to update a classically tailored suit (see my outfits left).

Fashion can be seen as mere fun, frippery and frivolity, but showing an interest in it and reflecting it to some degree in your appearance does have its serious side too. Research has shown that those who look current and contemporary are perceived to be equally up-to-date in their knowledge, thinking and attitudes. Within the workplace, home and social situations this can have profound effects on how others judge, react and relate to you often on a subconscious level. Looking *old-fashioned* can affect your own self-image, making you feel old, out of touch and boring; but, more importantly, you may be perceived in this way by others, with undesired results within your work and home life.

At What Age Should You Stop Following Fashion?

Never. Fashion has nothing to do with age and everything to do with attitude of mind and an interest in the times in which you live. Young children today can have fun keeping up with trends in an inexpensive way with cheap accessories and small items of clothing – even baby- and toddler-wear today reflects the same themes seen on the catwalk. If 1970s' styles come back into fashion, a fuller-figured woman in her sixties may not be able to wear cropped tops or hipster jeans, but an embroidered tunic and drawstring trousers will still echo the theme, look equally fashionable and be appropriate to her body shape and age. So whether you are young, middle-aged or more mature you can always follow fashion – just keep your own 'blueprint' of line, colour and fashion-personality in mind when you go shopping.

Having said that, there are some aspects of appearance which are very ageing and which should be noted by older women who may be taking attention away from their fashionable clothes.

The Six Sins of Seniority
Hair

Long hair can be extremely ageing as it exaggerates and accentuates the downward lines which occur on the face as we get older especially near the eyes, nose and mouth. A short outward or upward hairstyle gives an instant face-lift without surgery!

Too dark hair gives the complexion a drained and greyish look. Dyeing your hair to a dark shade when you are older will only look good if you have a deep complexion. As hair goes grey, pigment is also lost from the skin and eyes, and this effect will simply be accentuated by too intense a hair colour.

Tightly permed hair is far too harsh for older faces and is one of the most ageing factors of all. Tight perms only look really good on young, fresh faces – mature women will find a short style with softness and volume far more flattering.

Whether you are young, middle-aged or more mature, you can always follow fashion if you keep the blueprint of your own bodyline, colour and fashion-personality in mind.

Yellow-grey hair often results when hair which was originally quite warm finally goes grey but does not lose all its carotene. Silver-grey or white hair (which is all cool) can look striking, positive and dynamic, but yellow-grey (with its confusion of warm and cool shades) often looks dowdy and dull. Colouring the hair to a warm brown or honey-blonde brings life and vitality back to the colouring.

Upper Arms

If these are slack or flabby they are always ageing. Lifting tins of baked beans up and down above your head can help tone up the muscles here considerably if done on a regular basis! Alternatively, simply stick to elbow-length or three-quarter-length sleeves in summer and invest in shawls and wraps for strappy summer or evening dresses. Loose chiffon jackets are better than sarongs as beach cover-ups.

Bosoms

Those that rest on the waistline are extremely matronly, but they only need a well-fitting bra to give a better, more youthful silhouette. Many older women don't buy new bras 'because no

Left: A modern haircut, contemporary jewellery and updated make-up colours can take years off your age.

one sees them' – everyone, however, sees the effects of old or ill-fitting bras. As 90 per cent of women wear the wrong size bra, make sure you are measured for new ones. In my work training Personal Shoppers for leading high street retailers, I have found that with a correctly fitting bra some customers' shapes change from Straight to Tapered or even from Tapered to Curved.

Too Tight Clothes

Like tight perms these are best left to the young. Aim for an elegantly loose fit – you should be able to turn a skirt around your body; fit two fingers into the waistband of your trousers; and pull out 2 inches of fabric on each side of a blouse; your pleats should lie flat; and zips and buttons should not pull or gape open. Larger sizes of clothing make you look younger, slimmer and more elegant – simply cut out the label if you don't like the size that it shows!

Matching Accessories

Definitely a thing of the past, these will always show your age. Older women often opt for, say, a red bag, red hat, red gloves and red shoes, which looks dated and contrived. Some accessories can match each other (perhaps just two), but others can be the same colour as the outfit.

Shoes

Your shoes can make or break an outfit, and older women often commit their biggest mistakes with footwear. It goes without saying that old-fashioned shoes will ruin a contemporary outfit, but even a current shoe can look bad in the wrong colour. The basic rule is that shoes should be the same intensity or darker than the hemline, but older women often wear shoes much lighter than their hemline – cream, beige or even white. White shoes only look good with a white skirt or trousers, or with an outfit where white is the predominant colour in a patterned fabric.

How Do You look Good in Swimwear?

Fashions in swimwear do not change so frequently as they do with other garments. Finding the perfect swimsuits for your shape and proportions is essential for confidence at the beach and swimming pool, and thankfully you can keep them for years if you invest in a good make. Look back at Chapter 3 to see which figure proportion boxes you ticked. Below are the solutions to the proportions which cause most problems when wearing a swimsuit or bikini.

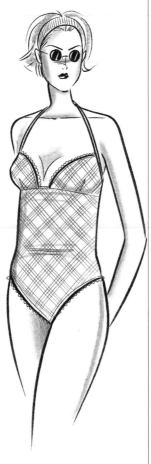

Broad Shoulders

Wide shoulders are definitely good news for swimsuit wearers, particularly if you carry your weight on the bottom half of your body, as your shoulders will help balance and slim down your hips/tum/bum. If you feel your shoulders are too big and beefy, however, avoid very wide-set straps or any kind of shoulder details such as bows or buttons.

Solutions

Halter neck-style suits are the best to slim down big shoulders, as the diagonal line created across each shoulder will visually slice it in two. Deep necklines are also good to draw the eye downwards. Tie your sarong in a halter neck style also.

Narrow Shoulders

In the 1980s, the era of 'power dressing', even swimwear and bras were designed with tiny shoulder-padded straps which were a godsend to those blessed with narrow or sloping shoulders! Until they come back into fashion again, you have to deceive the eye into widening your shoulders and diminishing your bottom half with tricks of colours and line. Above all, avoid halter necks whose straps just follow the line of the sloping shoulder and emphasize it.

Solutions

Wide-set shoulder straps are best, on a suit which has a highish neckline, a light colour on top and a darker shade on the bottom. Tie your sarong horizontally under your arms to broaden your upper half.

Right: High-waisted bikinis are ideal to camouflage a big tum or big hips – especially if fitted with a tummy control panel. Avoid bikinis if you are short-waisted, and opt for a one-piece swimsuit.

Large Bust

This problem is catered for very well in swimwear with many styles now being available in cup sizes and with underwiring or 'shelf' bras inside. Above all, avoid swimsuits in flimsy fabrics, with thin straps and no bust support at all – this leaves your breasts squashed flat perilously near your waistline!

Solutions

Underwires and broad straps will give you good support but also try designs which have a 'wrap-over' effect or any kind of diagonal patterning across the bust area. Alternatively, a suit with a deep colour in the bra area, becoming lighter below, will also help slim down your bust. Tie your sarong around the hips and never across or directly on top of the bust.

Small or No Bust

A recent survey has shown that 13 per cent of women have an A-cup bra size, many of these being slim or petite women. However, a small bust need not be a very big problem in swimwear.

Solutions

You can easily wear an unwired, tank-style swimsuit, but if you want your bust to look larger and fuller choose styles with underwired cups and padding – some pads are removable, to give you a choice of how much cleavage you wish to create! Twisted or bandeau-style tops, without straps, look good and add a little more substance to the bust area. Ruffles, gathers, texture, horizontal patterns and bright colours also have a bust-enhancing effect, particularly if the suit is plain and dark below the bustline.

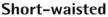

Short-waisted

If you only have a small distance between your waist and bust, a bikini will simply emphasize this fact and make you look much wider around your waist and ribcage. For a slimmer look you need to create the illusion of a longer midriff. Avoid all horizontal waistline details on swimsuits, especially belts.

Solutions

A one-piece suit which is underwired to lift your bust as high as possible is essential. Any kind of vertical line – pattern, seaming or buttons – will also help to lengthen the torso. Swimsuits made up from different coloured vertical panels are excellent and will also make your waist look slimmer if the panels curve inwards. Tie your sarong under your arms to slim and lengthen your body.

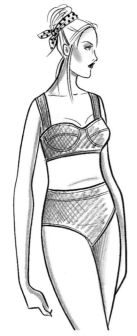

Big Hips/Tum/Bum

This is the biggest problem area for most women and the one they usually feel most self-conscious about. It is essential to avoid swimsuits in light and/or shiny fabrics, as these can increase the size of your protruding belly, ample derrière or love-handle hips by several inches in each area! Any kind of waist-emphasis, belts or horizontal details on the bottom half should be avoided too.

Solutions

A one-piece swimsuit with a tummy-control panel can have girdle-like slimming power. A deep, matt fabric on the bottom half is good, and any kind of vertical or diagonal pattern will help slim the area down. Draw the attention upwards with lighter or brighter shades on the top half, and opt for wide-set shoulder straps to balance your upper and lower proportions. Skirted styles can look good if you have broad shoulders and if the skirt is long enough to hang downwards and not outwards! Tie your sarong at an angle across the stomach with the knot low on the hip to create a strong diagonal line across the lower body.

Petite/Short Legs

If you are short it is best to avoid horizontally striped swimsuits as the lines will make you look even shorter and wider. If your legs are very short, avoid low-cut legs or 'shorts-style' swimsuits which can visually reduce your leg length by several inches.

Solutions

A swimsuit with strong vertical lines or patterns is best to give the illusion of extra height. A high-cut leg will make your legs look longer, but if your hips/thighs are overweight unsightly bulges can result. A medium-cut leg is the best solution, worn with sandals with a moderate, chunky heel. Tie your sarong around the neck, halter-style, or under the arms for a lengthening look. Avoid sarongs with border patterns at the hem-line.

Fuller Figure

If you are fuller-figured (especially if you are short as well) you don't want anything that makes you look any shorter or wider.

Solutions

It is essential to have a well-fitting swimsuit – particularly one which is not too small. You will probably need to buy one a size bigger than your dress size. If you don't like the size on the label, just cut it out – no one will know. Fuller figures always look better in a swimsuit in a deep, muted colour and a matt fabric. A medium-cut leg is best and built-in tummy panels give girdle-like control to your middle. Underwired cups are essential, as is a high Lycra content (but not shiny). Look for plenty of vertical or diagonal details such as pattern, seams or panels, wide straps and a lowish neckline.

How Do You Choose and Wear a Hat?

Hats, when selected and worn correctly, can look fantastic, get you noticed, boost your confidence and immediately make a plain outfit look stunning. From Chapter 2 you should know whether you are looking for a softer or more angular shape, but when shopping for hats also bear the following guidelines in mind.

The Full Picture

When choosing a hat it is extremely important to see yourself in a full-length mirror to gauge its scale in relation to your full body. If you are petite and and/or small-boned, you will then see immediately how an over-large hat can make you look like a standard lamp! Petite women should never have a hat brim wider than their shoulders. Conversely, a fuller-figured or large-boned woman can see how a very small hat will instantly turn her into a Stan Laurel. If the hat department in the shop only has a head-and-shoulders mirror, take your choice of hats to the dress department for a full-length view.

A Firm Fit

Apart from some decorative fashion hats which perform a precarious balancing act, most practical, everyday hats should wedge firmly on the head and be in no danger of blowing away with the first puff of wind. If a hat fits properly, you should be able to feel the top of your head in the top of the crown; the hat should not fall off if you put your head upside down; and the sides or crown should not be wider than the sides of your face. Hat pins can be used to secure a hat to your hair, but today these are more decorative than practical.

Far right: A hat can make a plain outfit look stunning!
Right: A hat worn down to your eyebrow improves your posture, elongates your neck and boosts your confidence.

Hats Versus Hair

You should always consider how you will be wearing your hair when choosing a hat, as this can affect the best style and sometimes the fit. It is usually better not to have long hair showing beneath a *formal* hat, as this can have a dragging-down effect as well as spoiling the impact of the hat. Long hair (past shoulder length) looks more stylish worn up (in which case, you may need a larger size of hat) or tied back. On the whole, a short (above shoulder-length), neat style looks better with a formal hat. However, *casual* hats such as fur, straw and knitted ones can look good with long hair, particularly if you are tall (see left).

Perfect Posture

A hat worn correctly can make a huge difference to your appearance. Many woman wear their hats very gingerly on the back of their head, rather like a halo! When you put the hat on, you should pull it right down to your eyebrows until you can only see your feet. This means that, in order to see where you are going, you need to lift your head, which in turn elongates your neck, pushes back your shoulders and magically adds several inches to your height. Many women wrongly assume that a hat is a very 'shortening' accessory to wear, but the right hat worn correctly is a boost to both stature and confidence.

New
Directions

What a Difference a Day Makes

Now it's time to see all the theory put into practice with some more-than-willing make-over volunteers. All the women featured in this chapter had sent me full-length and head/shoulders photos of themselves and filled in my very detailed application form so that I could analyze their face, figure, proportions and colouring. I also asked for some brief details on their lifestyle, wardrobe needs and fashion personality to make sure I didn't choose anything for them which was wildly out of character or totally inappropriate!

Vivianne Ayres

Clothes Encounters

Some of our ladies had risen at the crack of dawn to travel to London for the makeover shoot (hence some very tired eyes in the 'Before' photos!) but after a welcoming cup of coffee (or two) and some hot croissants it was down to work and time to start trying on the clothes. I always select three or four outfits, based on the person's particular style blueprint that I have worked out, so that they too have an element of choice and can ultimately feel comfortable in their final outfit.

Every woman's dream come true – a day with the experts to go from 'Before' (left) to 'After' (above).

Hair Today – Gone Tomorrow

Next stop on the agenda is a chat with top hairdresser Paul Falltrick, to discuss face shape and the texture, colour and cut of the present style to see what, if any, changes are necessary. Sometimes it's a case of adding highlights to brighten a dull colour or lowlights to create depth and volume expertly applied by Paul's assistant, Jenny Pringle. Sometimes more curve in the hair is needed to complement soft features or a sharper or straighter style is needed to complement angular bone structure. A rinse may be necessary to cover the odd grey hair and sometimes the whole lot just has to come off!

Colour Me Gorgeous

When the hair is almost finished (and you've nearly got over the shock) it's time to relax and be pampered with a full, colour cosmetic makeover. My leading make-up artist, Michelle Attlesey, and myself pencilled, powdered, concealed and accentuated to make the very most of all the different Colour Directions which our volunteers presented. When make-up is perfect, the final finishing touches are made to the hair.

Lights! Camera! Action!

After lunch (and a couple of glasses of wine to steady the nerves for the main photo session) it's time to select the final bits and pieces – jewellery, shoes, scarves, belts, glasses and sunglasses – and then step onto the spot-lit stage for a modelling debut. By this time, I feel very bedraggled – anyone good at makeovers?

Carol   Val   Sue   Kathy   Elaine   Linda   Pat   Paula...   and Paul

Makeover 1– Sue

> **Name:** Susan Juru **Age:** Early 40s
> **Face Direction:** Rectangular outline with mainly angular features
> **Figure Direction:** Straight
> **Proportions:** Large bust, broad shoulders, petite (5' 4")
> **Colour Direction:** Bright (brown hair, blue eyes, fair skin)
> **Needs:** To update her look from the one she's had for years.

STYLE DIRECTIONS

Clothes

Susan arrived in a grey trouser suit which was actually very modern and a good shape for her Straight Figure Direction. Her bright colouring, however, needed some contrast around the face – a bright shirt, scarf, or patterned blouse. Susan was, however, willing to try a 'totally bright' look and looked stunning in the red suit with contrasting black buttons and zebra-pattern shirt. Being petite (and having fantastic legs!), Susan looked great in the short skirt with toning tights and shoes. No emphasis was placed on the bust or waist/ribs area to keep attention focused on the face and legs.

Hair

Yes, it all came off! Being petite and small-boned, Susan was swamped by her very long hair. A brown rinse was applied to cover a few grey hairs and the new short style showed off her wonderful bone structure which was further emphasized by the sharp neckline and angular earrings.

Colour Cosmetics

Vanilla and purple eye shadows, charcoal eyeliner, black mascara, rose blusher and red lipstick.

Susan's Comments

66 *I feel fantastic –
but will my husband
recognize me?* 99

Makeover 2 – Pat

Name: Pat Sharp   **Age:** Early 60s
Face Direction: Rectangular outline with mostly angular features
Figure Direction: Short neck, big hips/tum/bum, petite (5' 4")
Colour Direction: Cool (silver hair, blue eyes, fair skin)
Needs: To look more modern – but not too dowdy!

STYLE DIRECTIONS
Clothes

Pat arrived in a grey, knitted skirt suit with a matching
tunic top. Although grey is a good colour for her
wardrobe, Pat needs to brighten it with some other cool
colours to prevent a 'top-to-toe' greyish look which can be
quite ageing. Because Pat has a short neck, she needs a
lower neckline to give the illusion of a longer, slimmer
neck. Also she is best avoiding pattern around her
hips/tum/bum (such as the one around her sweater) to
keep attention away from that area. Pat was willing to try
a soft, modern trouser suit as an alternative to her usual
skirt suits, which gives a current, contemporary look
without being too trendy! A long, chiffon scarf (not tied at
the neck) and modern jewellery completed the look.

Hair

A sharper cut was recommended for Pat with 'points' in
front of the ears to complement the angles of her face.
Much of the fullness was taken out the sides to lessen
the 'rounded' look of the style. Some dark lowlights were
also added to the silver shade to add depth and volume.

Colour Cosmetics:

Pink and purple eye shadows, taupe eyebrow pencil,
black/brown mascara, pink blusher and fuchsia lipstick.

Pat's Comments

❝ I feel 20 years younger and full of life – or is that the effects of the champagne? ❞

Makeover 3 – Kathy

Name: Kathy George	**Age:** Early 30s
Face Direction: Oval with mainly soft features	
Figure Direction: Tapered	
Proportions: Short-waisted, big hips/tum/bum, average height (5' 7')	
Colour Direction: Light (blonde/light brown hair, blue eyes, fair skin)	
Needs: To find an outfit for a forthcoming wedding which can be worn afterwards.	

STYLE DIRECTIONS

Clothes

Kathy arrived in a semi-fitted navy blouse and navy trousers which were quite good for her Tapered Figure Direction – the light buttons on the blouse even made a connection with her light colouring! For Kathy's forthcoming wedding we chose a princess-line shift dress with matching jacket in a pale blue and taupe patterned brocade which was perfect for her shape and colouring. After the event the dress could be worn with a simple cream, taupe or pale blue cardigan and sandals for a more 'dressed-down' look; the jacket would look great over Kathy's own navy blouse and trousers (in which she arrived) for an even more casual look. Silver earrings with a central pale blue stone completed her 'dressed up' look.

Hair

As she has an oval face, Kathy luckily suits lots of different hairstyles but she needs to keep the shape soft to complement her features. As we felt that a cut was not necessary, some extra blonde highlights were added to Kathy's hair and it was set on large rollers to give a fuller, more glamorous look for the event.

Colour Cosmetics

Pink and taupe eye shadows, blonde eyebrow pencil, brown eyeliner and mascara, dusky pink blusher and lipstick.

Kathy's Comments

66 *I wouldn't have dreamt that this outfit could be worn in different ways – great ideas.* 99

Makeover 4 – Paula

Name: Paula Galloway	**Age:** Early 30s

Face Direction: Heart shaped with mainly soft features.

Figure Direction; Curved

Proportions: Long neck, long-waisted, average height (5' 6')

Colour Direction: Deep/Muted (black hair, brown eyes, dark skin)

Needs: To find a sexy outfit for the Millennium celebrations but not a short dress with bare arms or plunging neckline.

STYLE DIRECTIONS

Clothes

Paula arrived wearing a sweat top and jogging pants (plus a beret which looked very cool but we had to remove it for the 'Before' photo to see her hair). Beneath these comfortable but shapeless clothes (Paula likes to be comfortable) we discovered the most fantastic, curvy, hourglass figure of almost model-like proportions! My choice had to be a designer, tuxedo evening suit with a very fitted jacket and slim-leg trousers. This was teamed with high evening shoes and a see-through, lace/beaded evening top which showed off her trim waistline and long ribcage superbly. The final finishing touch was a pair of diamante drop earrings – any more jewellery would have distracted from the beaded top.

Hair

Paula's hair was extremely short, a cut was completely out of the question. Our hairdresser added some golden highlights to the front to increase Paula's muted/warm tones. For a fun party look, Paula was persuaded to try a long, full wig – the result was stunning!

Colour Cosmetics

Gold and chocolate eye shadows, black eyeliner and mascara, brown eyebrow pencil, spice blusher, toffee lipstick.

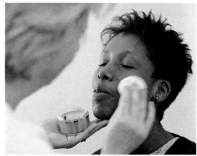

Paula's Comments

66 *I love this outfit – it manages to be both fun and sophisticated.* 99

Makeover 5 – Linda

Name: Linda Holmes	**Age:** Late 40s
Face Direction: Diamond shape with mostly angular features	
Figure Direction: Curved	
Proportions: Long neck, small bust, average height (5' 5")	
Colour Direction: Muted (blonde hair, hazel eyes, medium complexion)	
Needs: To achieve a smart daytime look and discover her best colours.	

STYLE DIRECTIONS

Clothes

Linda arrived dressed head to toe in denim – her usual attire as a farmer's wife who spends much of her time working with horses. The style of her outfit was quite straight and, because of her Curved Figure Directions. She would do better to tuck her shirt into her jeans and wear a good, leather belt to show off her waist. For the smarter look she desired, I selected a taupe trouser suit which I teamed with brown strappy sandals, a brown leather belt (with shiny buckle to attract attention at the waist) and a patterned blouse which gave interest across her small bust. This would be a great outfit for lunch or dinner with friends but would look equally good 'dressed down' with a T-shirt or sweater and loafers.

Hair

Linda's hair is naturally curly which makes it conflict a little with her angular face. Both Paul Falltrick and I wanted to cut it very short to show off her bone structure – but we failed miserably as Linda had spent ages growing it! So her hair was blow-dried straight for a sleeker look. She would also suit it worn up.

Colour Cosmetics

Cream and brown eye shadows, brown eye pencil and mascara, beige blusher and mid-pink lipstick.

Linda's Comments

❝ *I have never worn this colour before and wouldn't have looked twice at it in the shops – I'm amazed; it looks fantastic.* ❞

Makeover 6 – Val

Name: Valerie Pearson	**Age:** Late 30s

Face Direction: Rectangular with mostly angular features
Figure Direction: Straight
Proportions: Broad shoulders, small bust, wide ribcage, average height (5' 6")
Colour Direction: Warm (red hair, hazel eyes, freckly skin)
Needs: To find the starting point of a capsule wardrobe for a summer holiday.

STYLE DIRECTIONS

Clothes

Valerie arrived in a T-shirt and track-suit bottoms – she is an ex-P.E. Teacher and currently works at a health and leisure suite. Her Straight Figure Direction is quite typical of an athletic woman – broad shoulders, small bust and flat hips/tum/bum. We decided, for a change, to give her a much softer romantic look for a holiday – but still in keeping with her Figure and Colour Direction.

I always advise choosing some patterned garments first when planning a capsule, as this gives you the colour scheme around which to work. The white T-shirt is not an ideal choice for Valerie's Warm colouring but creams, browns, oranges etc. are ideal. The chiffon two-piece dress looks great as a day or evening outfit but both pieces could be worn separately with other items. I would suggest a brown trouser suit and beige shorts suit as major additions plus other toning tops, bottoms, swimsuits and accessories.

Hair

Valerie's hair is naturally curly and so thick that it was 'crowding' her face and covering her great bone structure. Our hairdresser thinned it slightly and then pulled it with straightening irons away from the face.

Colour Cosmetics

Sand and teal eye shadows, light brown eyebrow pencil, ivy eye pencil, brown mascara, beige blusher and coral lipstick.

Valerie's Comments

66 *This is a real departure from my usual style which is normally sporty or tailored – I feel a different person.* 99

Makeover 7 – Elaine

Name:	Elaine Lee	**Age:**	Mid-40s

Face Direction: Square with mainly soft features

Figure Direction: Tapered

Proportions: Extra petite (5' 1"), small bust, short waisted

Colour Direction: Deep/Bright (black hair, black eyes, medium skin)

Needs: To move away from her safe, classic look and look more current.

STYLE DIRECTIONS

Clothes

Elaine arrived in a calf-length, straight, belted skirt and high buttoned, patterned blouse. Being Tapered, she looked a little bundled-up around her short ribcage and, being ultra-petite, her hemline was too close to the ground making her look even shorter. An above-the-knee dress revealed an amazing pair of legs which Elaine had kept hidden for many years! Her lovely slim ankles were also accentuated with thin-heeled shoes with a shiny buckle to draw attention. The semi-fitted dress with matching jacket gave only gradual waist emphasis and was much more flattering than the tucked-in top and belt. The final finishing touch to Elaine's new, contemporary look was a modern pendant-style necklace with matching, drop-earrings.

Hair

Oriental hair always looks great in a 'bob' style because it is so straight and thick. Paul Falltrick shortened the style, however, and curved the sides inwards to soften the squareness of Elaine's face and complement her soft features.

Colour Cosmetics

Pink and navy eye shadows, dark brown eyebrow pencil, navy eyeliner and mascara, rose blusher and red lipstick.

Elaine's Comments

❝ I have never worn red lipstick or such a short skirt but I love my new look. ❞

Makeover 8 – Angela

Name: Angela White	**Age** Early 20s

Face Direction: Round with mainly soft features

Figure Direction: Tapered

Proportions: Narrow shoulders, short waisted, average height (5' 5')

Colour Direction: Light (blonde hair, green eyes, fair skin)

Needs: To smarten up her look as she moves from a student to working life.

STYLE DIRECTIONS

Clothes

Angela arrived in a pale pink sweater and black trousers – this was quite a smart look for her as she has tended to live in trainers and snowboarding gear for the last few years! She was willing to try her first suit but it had to be modern (not frumpy!) and one which could be dressed up for evenings out. I chose a cream single-breasted suit with an above-the-knee skirt, rounded lapels to complement her soft features and slightly padded shoulders to balance her shoulders and hips. (Angela is a typical British pear!) For interviews this would look great with a semi-fitted, shirt and medium-heeled shoes. For evening we teamed it with a low-cut, stretchy lace top, snakeskin sandals and a silver, heart pendant.

Hair

As Angela has quite a round face she needs either height or length to elongate it slightly. For her evening look, we opted for an up-pinned style but kept it quite 'relaxed' with wispy pieces falling near her soft face.

Colour Cosmetics

Peach and biscuit eye shadows, taupe eye pencil, brown mascara, salmon blusher and beige lipstick.

Angela's Comments

66 *I feel so grown-up – this look will give me enormous confidence at interviews.* 99

Personal Style Directions

Look Your Best Ever with Carol Spenser's Mail-Order-Makeover. Like the makeover subjects in the previous chapter, you too can receive your individual fashion and beauty advice direct from Carol Spenser's office. For just £29.95, you will be provided with a personalized face and figure analysis, colour and make-up advice, a wardrobe guide and current fashion information. Join the exclusive group of women who have benefited from Carol's advice via her TV and magazine makeovers and this unique Personal Style Directions makeover pack.

How to Apply

To receive your Personal Style Directions pack, simply fill in a questionnaire giving details of your physical characteristics, colouring, bodyshape, figure proportions etc. You also need to send two recent photographs: a head-and-shoulders shot (to check your colouring/face shape/glasses etc.) and a full-length shot (to check your figure, proportions etc.). Your application form and photographs are analysed by Carol Spenser and her trained staff, who then produce your Personal Style Directions pack.

Your Personal Style Directions Pack will contain:
- Face Directions – suggestions for hairstyles, glasses, jewellery
- Figure Directions – guidelines for your best clothing shapes
- Proportional Problems – solved with easy-to-follow tips
- Colour Directions – perfect shades for your clothes and make-up
- Wardrobe Directions – to suit your shape and lifestyle
- Fashion Directions – over 50 pages of the latest fashions
- Colour Directions Wallet – a handy reminder of 'near face' colours
- Quality Lipstick – selected for your Colour direction

At only £29.95 Personal Style Directions is approximately $1/3^{rd}$ the price of a full style consultation – so, don't delay! Return the slip on page 160 to receive your application form.

Visit Our Website!

www.styledirections.com

- features
- advice
- products
- on-line ordering

Special Book Offers

As a valued purchaser of *Style Directions for Women*, you can receive Carol Spenser's other popular books at a reduced price direct from her office. Your books can also be signed by Carol on special request – if a personal message is required, please print it clearly on plain paper and attach it to the application form on page160.

Style Directions for Men

A companion book to *Style Directions for Women* (published Oct '99), this book will help smarten up the man in your life! Is he Triangular, Rectangular or Contoured?; are his features sharp or rounded?; does he need help with grooming or hairstyles?; advice on disguising a beer belly or sprucing up his image for work or weekends? Packed with colour photographs and illustrations, *Style Directions for Men* can put new life in your man or a new man in your life!
Hardback price **£15.99** (inc p+p) Normal price £17.99 – save £2.00.
Paperback price **£11.99** (inc p+p) Normal price £12.99 - save £1.00.

Wedding Style Counsel

Carol Spenser's second book (published July '96) is an indispensable read for every bride-to-be. Chapter by chapter, the book helps with every big decision of style – the wedding dress, headdress, flowers, lingerie, cosmetics, groom and attendants' outfits – plus guidelines for suits and hats for civil weddings, going away outfits and mothers of the bride and groom. This 160 page book, packed with colour photos, guarantees a stylish and perfectly co-ordinated wedding whatever your budget.
Price **£12.99** (inc p+p) normal price £15.99 – save £3.00

Petite Style Counsel

Carol Spenser's third book (published May '98) provides excellent style advice for all women under 5'4" – who now account for 42% of the UK female population. Packed full of invaluable hints and tips on how to look (and feel!) an extra few inches taller, this book covers all aspects of style from hairstyles and handbags to swimsuits and sarongs. A big buy for little women!
Price **£4.99** (inc p+p) Normal price £5.99 – save £1.00

Slimline Style Counsel

Carol Spenser's fourth book (published May '98) shows you how to look slimmer without going on a crash diet! The average dress size in the UK is now size 16 and the average cup size of a bra is now a D-cup. The female figure has changed from the 'hour-glass' of the 40s and 50s to a straighter, stronger shape that needs a new style of dressing. Learn how to flatter your figure whether you're a size 14 or 24.
Price **£4.99** (inc p+p) Normal price £5.99 – save £1.00

Order form

Cut out or photocopy this form and send to:
Style Directions,
Mendham Watermill, Mill Lane, Mendham,
Harleston, IP20 0NN.

Name ....

Address ....

....

....

Post code ....

Tel No. ....

Please send me (tick boxes)

❑ **Personal Style Directions pack**
£29.95

❑ **Style Directions for Men**
Price £15.99 hbk ❑   £11.99 pbk ❑

❑ **Wedding Style Counsel**
Price £12.99

❑ **Petite Style Counsel**
Price £4.99

❑ **Slimline Style Counsel**
Price £4.99

❑ Details of Style and Colour Courses
Free

Total amount £_____

❑ I enclose a cheque*

❑ I wish to pay by Access/Visa/Mastercard

No [ ][ ][ ][ ][ ][ ][ ][ ][ ][ ][ ][ ][ ][ ][ ][ ][ ][ ]

Expires end . . . .

Signature . . . .

* Please make cheques payable to Style Directions.

Products and Services

A wide range of products and services are available to the general public, image and colour consultants, and members of the fashion and beauty industries. These include Colour Directions swatch cards and wallets, Colour Directions capes, a quality range of Colour Cosmetics and current or back orders of the Fashion Directions booklets. Discounts are available for bulk orders on some products, and customers can be added to our credit-card mailing list to receive the Fashion Directions booklet on a twice yearly basis. Visit our website: www.styledirections.com to view our range of products.

Style and Colour Courses

If you would like to experience 'hands-on' advice from Carol Spenser or her team of trained consultants, 3-day style and colour workshops or week-long courses are available. You may want to treat yourself, you may be considering starting your own business or you may simply want to add an extra service to your existing business. Whatever your reason, certification from the UK's leading style company gives you a flying start.

Business Directions Seminars or personal consultations can be tailored to the specific needs of individual companies to ensure that all personnel, (male and female), are making the right impact. Special training programmes in the areas of Colour Directions and Personal Shopping can be devised for fashion and beauty retailers, and makeovers or personal consultations can be arranged as incentives or promotions for staff and customers.

For further information, please contact:
Style Directions,
Mendham Watermill, Mill Lane, Mendham,
Harleston, IP20 0NN
Tel: 01379 855410   Fax: 01379 855414
email: publicpersona@dial.pipex.com
Website: www. styledirections.com